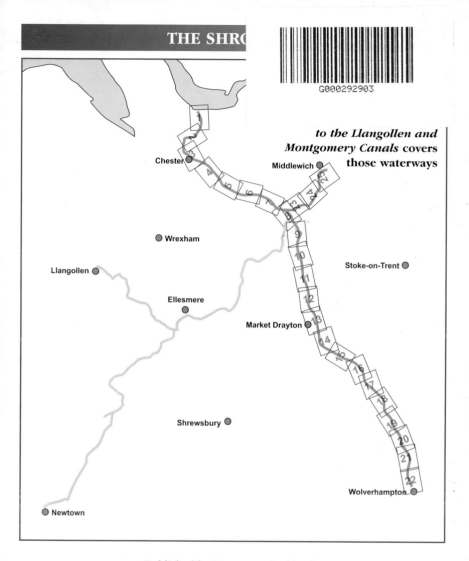

*to the Llangollen and Montgomery Canals* **covers those waterways**

Chester · Middlewich · Wrexham · Llangollen · Stoke-on-Trent · Ellesmere · Market Drayton · Shrewsbury · Wolverhampton · Newtown

G000292903

## Published by Waterways World Ltd,

151 Station Street, Burton-on-Trent, Staffordshire DE14 IBG, England.
Revised and Edited by Euan Corrie
Original Research by Julie Lloyd
Maps by Branch Out Design, Bretby, Burton-on-Trent

One of a series of guides covering the Inland Waterways of England and Wales

British Library Cataloguing in Publication Data
A catalogue record for this book is available from the British Library
ISBN 1 870002 46 6
Printed in the United Kingdom by Information Press, Oxford

# INTRODUCTION

This Guide covers in detail the Shropshire Union Canal between Autherley Junction on the northern outskirts of Wolverhampton and Ellesmere Port on the southern bank of the Mersey Estuary, together with its Middlewich Branch from Barbridge Junction near Nantwich to Middlewich.

This new edition has been thoroughly revised and everything that the first-time boat hirer or the already experienced navigator needs to know about the route that lies before him is included. It contains information about navigating the waterway, facilities for boating and shopping, and places of interest within walking distance of the canal. Moreover, towpath walkers and those who enjoy exploring canals by car are also catered for. So, whatever your interests are, we hope that you will find this guide useful. Have a good trip, remember the Country Code and enjoy discovering the Shropshire Union system.

## Acknowledgements

The editor is grateful to a great many people who have assisted in the production of this guide. In particular Julie Lloyd undertook the initial research; Philippa Corrie acted as boat captain, car navigator, clerk and secretary on subsequent trips. Thanks are also due to the staff of British Waterways and the Aylesbury Canal Society's Launderette List is, as always, an invaluable aid.

## A Brief History

What we today call the Shropshire Union Canal is, in fact, made up of four entirely separate canals, which, through various amalgamations, eventually became the Shropshire Union Canal in 1845. The four constituent canals, in order of construction, were: The Chester Canal from Chester to Nantwich opened in 1779; the Wirral Line of the Ellesmere Canal from Ellesmere Port to Chester opened in 1795; the Middlewich Branch of the Chester & Ellesmere Canal Company (an amalgamation of the aforementioned) opened between Barbridge Junction and Middlewich in 1833, and the Birmingham & Liverpool Junction Canal from Nantwich to Autherley Junction opened in 1835. These and other canal companies formed the Shropshire Union Canal Company, aiming to combat growing competition from the railways. But a year after that amalgamation of 1845, they retitled themselves the Shropshire Union Railways & Canal Company, and announced plans to convert much of their mileage from waterway to railway. Thankfully, such a drastic move never came to fruition, largely because in 1847 the SUR&CCo was acquired by the London & North Western Railway (LNWR), which was only too happy for the canals under its control to continue functioning in an area being developed by its arch rival the Great Western Railway.

It is interesting for today's pleasure boater to observe the differences in the construction methods employed by the constituents of the Shropshire Union. From Barbridge to Middlewich and from Autherley to Nantwich the canal was built to the designs of Thomas Telford, and shows itself to be a product of the later period of canal construction. Eschewing the contour-hugging predilections of

Euan Corrie

**All canal companies suffered from advances in technology, not only from the railways but also more directly as traction engines and other previously unimaginably heavy vehicles began to visit their property.**

earlier waterways, it cuts its way through hillsides and crosses valleys on embankments created by the spoil dug from the cuttings – a method which became known as the 'cut and fill technique' for obvious reasons. In contrast, the earlier Chester and Wirral canals tended to look for the easiest way through a landscape; meandering almost river-like around high ground.

Differences in use also made for variations that can still be noted now. The Chester and Wirral lines were built for use by barges known as Mersey flats; wide-beamed vessels which traded direct between the ports of Merseyside, Chester, Nantwich, and smaller wharves en route. On the other hand, the Birmingham & Liverpool Junction and the Middlewich Branch, were constructed for use by narrowboats of 7ft beam and, consequently, the locks and bridgeholes are on a much smaller scale. Differences in gauge such as these were instrumental in making canal transport unviable in the face of later competition. Yet, ironically, use of the versatile 25-ton capacity narrowboats outlasted that of flats carrying up to 60 tons on the northern part of the Shropshire Union.

In 1923 the SUR&CCo became, with the LNWR, part of the London Midland & Scottish Railway (LMS) as a result of the railway grouping. Again the Shropshire Union Canal escaped by the skin of its teeth when, in 1944, the LMS obtained an Act to close much of the SUC system including the waterways to Llangollen and Newtown in Wales and the canal from

Norbury Junction to Shrewsbury. Luckily, the main line survived to be nationalised in 1948. The 1950s saw the last regular cargoes carried on the Ellesmere Port–Barbridge Junction section in the shape of Thomas Clayton's colourful narrowboats transporting petroleum products to Oldbury near Birmingham, but commercial carrying continued between Autherley and Middlewich until the late 1960s. The 1950s was also a period of fierce campaigning for the 'Welsh' section of the system, not least by its engineer who wanted to use boats for maintenance. As a result the Llangollen Canal survives as a popular pleasure boating route included in the *Waterways World Guide to the Llangollen and Montgomery Canals*. The Montgomery Canal was closed after a breach in 1936 but is now the subject of progressive restoration works. The part of the system Shropshire Union extending down the locks at Norbury Junction into Shropshire has faired less well and only isolated remnants survive.

As the working narrowboats slowly disappeared from the main line, a new form of waterway traffic was growing up, and the scenic Shropshire Union Canal became a firm favourite with a new generation of pleasure boaters. In 1968 the canal was assured of a future when it was classified as a 'Cruiseway', which meant that its present owners, British Waterways, had a statutory duty to maintain it to cruising standards as prescribed in the Transport Act of that year.

## Licences

Addresses of all the authorities and organisations that can provide further information are listed on page 11.

All craft, whether powered or unpowered, including canoes and dinghies, must have a British Waterways Boat Licence when navigating the Shropshire Union Canal, or indeed, the rest of the connected canal system. Details of licensing are obtainable from the General Managers at Birmingham or Northwich or from British Waterways' Watford headquarters (see Useful Addresses on page 11).

### River Dee

Guidance for users of canal craft wishing to explore the river Dee is provided on page 24. Those heading upstream of Chester Weir will need to make arrangements with the BW General Managers' Office at Northwich (see Useful Addresses page 11) for use of the Dee Branch locks and also require a licence from Chester City Council to cover use of the 12 miles of attractive river to Farndon.

### Manchester Ship Canal

Craft must not enter the Manchester Ship Canal without first making arrangements with the Harbour Master's Department (see Useful Addresses page 11). Pleasure craft have a right of navigation on this large commercial waterway on payment of the toll, which may seem expensive for a single, non-stop, trip. The Manchester Ship Canal Company also lays down certain sensible requirements for the vessel. Most problematical may be that it will require a certificate signed by an approved surveyor that the vessel is fit for such a journey – often referred to as a 'Certificate of Seaworthiness' the requirements are not as stringent as the title infers. Other requirements as to equipment and insurance of the vessel will be detailed by the MSCCo when you apply. Hire companies may not permit the use of their craft on the Manchester Ship Canal. See also pages 13–16.

## Stoppages

From time to time, particularly in the winter months (November–March), it may become necessary for British Waterways to carry out maintenance work on the waterway. Alternatively, a dry spring or summer may result in restrictions due to shortage of water. Either of these circumstances may result in sections being closed or 'stopped'. Details of stoppages are published monthly in *Waterways World* magazine. For unscheduled stoppages telephone Canalphone North (01923 201401). To obtain assistance or report emergencies outside office hours dial 0800 4799947 for Freephone Canals. Have details of the waterway and the nearest lock or bridge number or similar landmark ready.

## Water

The Shropshire Union Canal is comparatively well blessed with water supplies. However, some boaters will consider this blessing a mixed one when contemplating the siting of Wolverhampton's large Barnhurst Sewerage Works and its relationship with the canal. However, the canal is shallow, and often stone paved, along its edges except at old wharves and recognised tying up places. No matter what the prevailing weather conditions all the water you use in locks has to be supplied from the reservoirs or pounds upstream so use it wiseley – CONSERVE IT! Share locks, if boat length or chamber width allows, wait for oncoming boats if the lock is in their favour (even if it costs you five minutes, that's better than a dry pound!) and always ensure that all the gates and paddles are closed before leaving a lock unless an approaching boat obviously intends to use it. There is no point in rushing into a short pound in the lock flights that is already occupied by a boat going in your direction – the water you empty from the lock will simply run over the weir to waste. Remember – 'One Up, One Down' saves water and time in the long run.

## Speed

There is a speed limit of 4mph on the canal. Even this low speed is often too fast. Remember – an excessive wash or breaking wave causes bank erosion and damage to moored craft as well as being a general nuisance. If the wash from the stern starts to break up the banks EASE OFF, and you'll probably find that your speed in relation to terra-firma will increase anyway. Slow down when approaching or passing moored craft, other craft under way, locks, bridges, tunnels, engineering works and on bends. When the view ahead is obstructed, slow down, sound your horn and listen.

## Rule of the Road

Craft meeting should steer to the right and pass each other left to left. If you do not intend to do this you must make it clear to the oncoming boat. When a vessel is being towed from the bank pass outside the vessel to avoid fouling the towing line – never pass between the towed vessel and the bank. Craft traveling with the current on rivers or tideway have the right of way over those heading against the flow.

## Depth

If you could see the canal drained of its water you'd be surprised how shallow it is, especially at the edges, the cross section being a shallow 'V' rather than 'U' shaped. Keep to the centre of the channel except when passing oncoming boats. This is particularly important on the large embankments south of Nantwich. Give way to larger craft, which require deeper water. You may find yourself aground if you have moved out of the centre channel to pass another boat. This is nothing to worry about. You should be able to reverse off, but if that doesn't work, push yourself off with your boat pole.

## Mooring

Always, unless specifically indicated to the contrary, moor against the towpath side of the canal. Steer your boat in bow first, put the engine into neutral and then pull the stern of your boat in with your rope. Keeping the propeller turning near to the bank could seriously damage the propeller and both the bed and bank of the canal. When pushing off again, ensure that the boat is well away from the bank before engaging forward gear.

Try to avoid using mooring spikes on the high embankments where any leaks they might encourage could be disastrous – mooring is prohibited in some places for this reason.

- *Do not* moor too near bridges or locks so as to obstruct full size craft cruising the canal.
- *Do not* moor on bends or in winding holes.
- *Do not* moor in the short pounds of a flight of locks.
- *Do not* stretch ropes across towpaths where they will obstruct and endanger towpath users.
- *Never* run your engine in gear when the boat is tied up, this rapidly erodes the bank and undermines even quite deep piling, not to mention creating a pile of silt in the middle of the channel a few yards astern. Apart from that it's against the canal bye-laws!

## Safety First

Remember always that prevention is better than cure. Wear non-slip footwear and beware of slippery lock sides and gates in wet weather. Beware of low bridges – some of which are lower in the middle (sometimes with supporting girders) than at each end. Make sure that your crew – especially those sitting on the cabin top – is aware of the presence of a low bridge. Before you enter a long tunnel, tell the crew to switch on the cabin lights (the cabin lights shining on the walls are useful to the helmsman). Ensure that torches are handy when entering tunnels and for use at night.

It is advisable to be able to swim when contemplating a holiday afloat. Non-swimmers and young children should wear life jackets. When walking along the side-decks hold the handrails on the cabin top.

Make sure that you know the position and method of operation of the fire extinguishers provided on the boat. Take a basic first aid kit with you including insect repellent. It is a good rule to spend the first night aboard making sure that you know where everything is, how emergency equipment works and reading the instructions or handbooks on essential equipment provided by the owner.

## Tunnels

Canal craft should be equipped with a suitable headlamp for navigating tunnels. This should be trained slightly to the right to avoid dazzling oncoming steerers in wide tunnels. Torches should also be carried. Go dead slow when approaching other craft but do not stop in tunnels except in an emergency.

There is only one tunnel on the Shropshire Union Canal, Cowley Tunnel, 81 yards long. It is wide enough for craft to meet within and has a towpath.

## Bridges

### Height

Some of the arched bridges have little headroom between cabin roof and brickwork. Boaters, particularly those with roof-top passengers, chimneys and tall pipes, are advised to look well ahead and play it safe rather than sorry!

### Lift Bridges

The nearest lift bridges are on the Llangollen Canal and are described in the *Waterways World Guide to the Llangollen and Montgomery Canals* almost all those on the Shropshire Union are fixed structures of one style or another. The exceptions are the Llangollen-style lift bridge on the Dee Branch (where you will be assisted by BW staff) and a powered swing bridge in Ellesmere Port Docks that will be operated for large craft by council staff.

Although visually often attractive, these lift bridges, like low brick arches, have

their own special hazards for navigators. If you line your boat up with the coping on the towpath side of the bridge, the roof of your boat should miss the bridge decking, but if the wind catches the boat, or the boat hits the coping and bounces off, you could hit your cabin. When approaching these bridges, never allow anyone to stand at the bows of the boat near to where the cabin might hit the bridge – several tons of boat travelling at up to 4mph could easily crush them between boat and bridge. Never attempt to get off the boat onto the deck of a moveable bridge, this has proved fatal several times.

Use common sense when lifting or swinging the bridges and do not open the bridge if a vehicle is approaching. Where no gate is provided, a member of your crew should warn road traffic.

**Note: Do not stand on the roof of the boat or anywhere along the gunwale nearest the bridge deck when passing under lift bridges and never attempt to get off the boat on to the bridge deck.**

## BW Sanitary Station keys
### (Yale type)

It is essential to have at least one of these on board to gain access to Sanitary Stations and water points. Keys are available for purchase direct from British Waterways (see under Useful Addresses on page 11) and from most boat yards and marinas.

## Mileage

| | |
|---|---|
| Ellesmere Port to Barbridge | $24^1/_2$ |
| Barbridge to Hurleston | $1^1/_4$ |
| Hurleston to Nantwich | 2 |
| Nantwich to Autherley | $38^3/_4$ |
| Barbridge to Middlewich | 10 |

## Locks
### Lock Dimensions

In canal parlance, the Birmingham & Liverpool Junction section of the

Shropshire Union from Nantwich to Autherley and the Middlewich Branch are known as narrow canals, meaning that the waterway, and more particularly the locks, were built to take the traditional English narrowboat.

Today, the lock dimensions are:

| | |
|---|---|
| Length | up to 72ft (21.9m) |
| Beam | up to 7ft (2.13m) |
| Headroom | 7ft (2.13m) |
| Draught | up to 3ft (0.91m) |

From Nantwich to Ellesmere Port or the river Dee the canal is 'wide' being designed for craft of up to 14ft beam. But these craft are excluded by the 11ft wide motorway bridges at Ellesmere Port and would in any case experience difficulty in some sections where the channel is not maintained to its original width.

## Number of Locks

| | |
|---|---|
| Ellesmere Port to Barbridge | 17 |
| Barbridge to Hurleston | 0 |
| Hurleston to Nantwich | 0 |
| Nantwich to Autherley | 29 |
| Barbridge to Middlewich | 3 |

## Lock Operation

The golden rule is never waste water. The lock drill described below should be followed systematically.

The basic principle of lock operation is that water never passes straight through a lock. It comes in from the top and stays in, or goes out through the bottom without any following it from the top. If you liken the lock itself to a kitchen sink – the top end to the tap and the bottom to the plug – don't turn the tap on until the plug is in, and don't pull the plug out until the tap is off.

## Lock Keepers

On the Dee branch and some major rivers and the Manchester Ship Canal lock keepers may be on hand to direct traffic and operate the lock. This is the exception; lock operation on canals is usually undertaken by the boat crew. At busy spots lock keepers may be available

to assist and regulate traffic. They may ask you to share a lock with another boat or wait whilst another boat comes through the other way. Obey their instructions but do not necessarily expect that they will do the work for you – that's part of the fun of your holiday.

## Staircase Locks

The only staircase locks on the part of the Shropshire Union system that is covered in this guide book are the pair at Bunbury and the three chamber set at Northgate in Chester. That at Grindley Brook is described in the *Waterways World Guide to the Llangollen and Montgomery Canals*.

A staircase lock is one where the top gate forms the bottom gate of the next chamber. These abound on the Leeds & Liverpool where they are often referred to as 'risers'. Staircase locks are basically the same as ordinary locks and there is only one rule: When you're going up always make sure that the chamber above you is full (so that its water can be used to fill your chamber) and when you're going down check that the chamber below you is empty (so that the water from your chamber can be let into it). Only open the paddles between one chamber and one of its immediate neighbours at a time so as not to drain all the water from under your boat and do not try to empty a higher chamber into one below which is already full!

Several staircases have full-time keepers to assist (but only Northgate has such welcome individuals and they only appear at peak times) so look for notices advising of their presence and take instructions before doing anything. In wide staircase locks you can sometimes pass a boat already coming from the opposite direction but plan the move with the other crew and make sure that everybody is conversant with the complications this will cause before attempting it.

## How to Operate Locks

A windlass is usually required to fit the paddle spindles of manually operated locks. These will usually be provided on

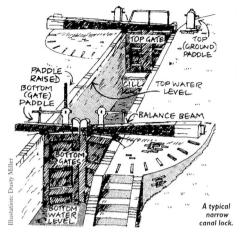

Illustration: Dusty Miller

A typical narrow canal lock.

the boat and have two holes of different sizes to take the spindle's squared end. Take care to use the correct sized hole on the spindle as a bad fit is dangerous since the windlass may fly off. In direct contravention of the recommendation of its own paddle gearing committee British Waterways has fitted a mixture of sizes of spindles at numerous locks so constant attention is needed. Do not leave the windlass on the spindle when not winding the paddle up or down – make sure the pawl (catch) is in place to stop the paddle falling and remove the windlass so that it cannot fly round if the catch slips.

Those of the crew who operate the paddles must remember that the noise of the engine and rushing water will prevent people on the boat hearing their instructions, or them hearing shouts of panic. Those ashore are responsible for keeping an eye on the boat all the time that the lock is filling or emptying to see that it continues to rise or fall steadily. If there is any doubt shut all the paddles quickly and then stop to think and check if the boat or its ropes

and fenders are catching on any part of the lock or other boats. Particularly check that the stem fender does not catch under the top gate or its handrails when going uphill. Boats sharing locks, which is a good way to save water, must lie beside or ahead and astern of one another, *never* twisted across each other at bow or stern. Like that they will jam as the level alters.

### (1) Going Uphill – Lock Empty

- Check that top paddles are closed.
- Enter the lock and drive the boat to the far end where there will be less turbulence as the lock fills.
- Close the bottom gates. See that the bottom gate paddles are closed.
- Open top ground paddles (where applicable). Water from these will pass under the boat to the other end of the chamber and hold the boat steadily against the top gate or cill.

Ropes are not usually required to hold a boat steady in narrow locks but will often be a good idea in bigger chambers. A line used as a spring running slightly astern from the fore end may be best with some tension being maintained by keeping the engine running in forward gear. Do not tie knots in any rope used in locks, they will jam when it is necessary to adjust the length of line as the water rises or falls and leave the boat hanging in mid air or sunk. Do not try to hold a rope as the lock fills either; take a couple of turns round a cleat or bollard and the extra friction thus

Illustration: Dusty Miller

gained will help prevent the boat dragging the rope through your hand causing nasty burns as it does so.

In most wide beam locks, such as those on the Chester Canal section north of Nantwich, where two or more narrowboats will fit alongside one another, a less turbulent ascent for a single boat will result from drawing the top ground paddle on the same side as the boat first. The water will usually pass beneath the boat and help to hold it steadily against the wall. But take extra care and read the notes on page 30 before putting two craft into Beeston Iron Lock.

In all cases only open the top gate paddles when their outlets in the gates are submerged (where applicable). Some locks have only gate paddles and greater care is needed here to avoid flooding the fore end of the boat by opening these too much too rapidly when going up hill.

- When the lock is full open the top gates.
- Leave the lock. Close the top gates and all paddles.

## (2) Going Uphill – Lock Full

- Check that there is no boat approaching above the lock which could save water by descending as you empty the lock for your boat to enter.
- If not, close the top gates. See that the top gate and ground paddles are closed.
- Open the bottom paddles.
- When the lock is empty open the bottom gates and close the bottom gate paddles. Proceed as (1) above.

## (3) Going Downhill – Lock Full

- Enter the lock and drive the boat to the far end where it will be well clear of the cill near the top gates as the water drops.
- Close the top gates. See that the top gate paddles and ground paddles are closed.
- Open the bottom gate paddles.
- When lock is empty open the bottom gates.
- Leave the lock. Close all bottom paddles and gates.

## (4) Going downhill – Lock Empty

- Check that there is no boat approaching below the lock which could save water by ascending as you fill the lock for your boat to enter.
- Close the bottom gates. See that the bottom gate paddles are closed.
- Open the top ground paddles.
- Open the top gate paddles when submerged (where applicable).
- When the lock is full, open the top gates. Proceed as (3) above.

Before leaving a lock see that all paddles are fully and securely closed. On canals it is important to shut the exit gates as well; failure to do so may result in serious flooding of property, stranding of craft through loss of water from the pound above, and possible flooding of craft when the pound is refilled.

It is easiest to pick up lock crew at the lock mouth, which saves approaching the shallow canal margins where you may run aground. But in all situations where crew are joining or leaving even a slowly moving boat make them get on or off at the stern. Should they slip they will then get wet after the boat has passed and not fall in where it will pass over them or crush them against a wall. At the stern the steerer is also at hand to put the engine out of gear quickly and assist.

## Beyond The Towpath

This publication is intended primarily as a guide to the canal but it also includes information on some of the places of interest near the canal. More detailed information can be obtained from local tourist offices. (See the text accompanying the maps and pages 11–12 for details of Tourist Offices).

## Walking The Shropshire Union Canal

Although canal towpaths are not usually Public Rights of Way, the public is now encouraged to make use of these excellent long-distance footpaths. Some very good canalside walks may be enjoyed by combining lengths of towpaths with the official footpaths and bridleways marked on the appropriate OS Landranger 1:50,000 maps covering the area. Many of these tracks and byways are also marked on the maps in this guide.

The towpath will generally be found to be in excellent condition throughout. Bear in mind however, the towpath is not a tarmac path in your local park and strong footwear will be needed in rural areas. The bottom of the spectacular cuttings can be spectacularly wet after adverse weather. Whilst it is perfectly feasible to use the SUC as a long-distance traffic-free footpath, perhaps most will find more enjoyment from planning shorter 3–5 mile walks along lengths of special interest or scenic value, such as Tyrley to Market Drayton, Audlem to Adderley or Bunbury to Beeston.

Where fences or gates cross the path walkers should leave them as they find them.

Though 'lock-wheeling' is as much part of today's boating as it was in the days of working boats, it is an offence to cycle along the towpath without a permit. These are obtainable from British Waterways local General Managers' offices or from BW's Head Office. There are some lengths of towpath where cycling is not permitted, details of which will be sent to applicants along with their free permit which must be displayed on handlebars at all times. Cyclists without a permit are liable to a fine.

Similarly, it is an offence to ride a horse along the towpath.

### General

Always respect the pleasure of other waterway users and the life of the countryside generally. Do not litter or pollute the waterways and always observe the Country Code:

- Guard against fire risks.
- Fasten all gates.
- Keep dogs under proper control.
- Keep to the paths across farm land.
- Avoid damaging fences, hedges and walls.
- Protect wildlife, wild plants and trees.
- Go carefully on country roads.

## Bibliography

*The Canals of the West Midlands* by Charles Hadfield. Published by David & Charles. An historical account including a chapter on the Shropshire Union.

*Narrow Boat* by L.T.C. Rolt. Originally published by Eyre & Spottiswoode, 1944. New edition republished by Alan Sutton, Gloucester, 1994. Unequalled in canal literature. A 1939 voyage through the canals of the Midlands taking in the Middlewich Branch and much of the main line of the Shropshire Union Canal.

*Thomas Telford* by L.T.C. Rolt. Published by Longman. A Full and readable, but long out-of-print biography.

*Thomas Telford* by Bracegirdle & Miles. Published by David & Charles. An illustrated outline of Telford's engineering achievements.

*Thomas Telford* by Rhoda Pearce. Published by Shire Publications. An inexpensive paperback outlining Telford's career.

*Thomas Telford's Aqueducts on the Shropshire Union Canal* by Ron Quenby. Published by Swan Hill Press. An illustrated history of the aqueducts, large and small, throughout the Shropshire Union system.

*Shroppie Boats* by Mike Webb. Published by J. M. Pearson & Son. Pictorial booklet depicting working narrowboats on the Shroppie.

*King's England Guide to Cheshire* by Arthur Mee. Somewhat dated but eminently readable.

*Waterways World* magazine: many articles on various aspects of the Shroppie have been published in the monthly magazine *Waterways World* – details of which may be found in the magazine's indexes. Indexes and backnumbers of *Waterways World* are available by post from Waterways World Ltd, 151 Station Street, Burton-on-Trent, Staffordshire DE14 1BG. (01283 742970).

## Maps and Charts

*GEOprojects Map of the Shropshire Union Canal* – fold-out boater's map.

Ordnance Survey maps (Landranger Series) 1:50,000 scale: sheets *117 Chester, Wrexham & Ellesmere Port, 118 Stoke-on-Trent & Macclesfield* and *127 Stafford & Telford* and, but not essentially, *139 Birmingham* cover the waterways described in this guide.

Note: British Waterways publish a range of information leaflets – copies of these may be obtained (free) from BW's Birmingham and Northwich offices – see under Useful Addresses, below.

## Waterways World Guides to adjoining canals

This guide links up with others in the series at:
1. Autherley Junction – the *Waterways World Guide to the Staffs & Worcs Canal*.
2. Hurleston Junction – the *Waterways World Guide to the Llangollen and Montgomery Canals*. (New edition in 2004.)
3. Middlewich – the *Waterways World Guide to the Trent & Mersey and Caldon Canals*. (New edition in 2004.)

**Other guides in this series:**
*Grand Union* (in two volumes: Birmingham to Northampton and Northampton to the Thames).
*Oxford Canal*
*Kennet & Avon Canal*
*Coventry, Oxford and Ashby Canals* (including the Birmingham & Fazeley).
All are available from: Waterways World Ltd, 151 Station Street, Burton-on-Trent, Staffordshire DE14 1BG (01283 742970).

## Useful Addresses

**British Waterways General Managers**
Shropshire Union Canal, north of Bridge 74, including the Middlewich Branch: Navigation Road, Northwich, Cheshire CW8 1BH (01606 723800, Fax 01606 871471).
Shropshire Union Canal, south of Bridge 74: Albert House, Quay Place, 92–93 Edward Street, Birmingham B1 2RA (0121 200 7400, Fax 0121 200 7401).
**British Waterways (Headquarters and Craft Licensing)** Willow Grange, Church Road, Watford, Hertfordshire WD17 4QA (01923 226422, email: enquiries@britishwaterways.co.uk).
Web site: www.britishwaterways.co.uk

**Manchester Ship Canal Company**
Harbour Master's Department, Manchester Ship Canal Co, Queen Elizabeth II Dock, Eastham, Wirral, Cheshire CH62 0BB (0151 327 1461, Fax 0151 327 6278, www.shipcanal.co.uk).

**Chester City Council**
Business Development Unit, Community Services, Chester City Council, The Forum, Chester CH1 2HS (01244 402267/402319, Fax 01244 348405, email: chestercitycouncil@chestercc.gov.uk).

## Tourist Information

**Chester** Town Hall, Northgate Street, Chester CH1 2HJ (01244 402111, Fax: 01244 400420, www. chestertourism. com).
Chester Visitor & Craft Centre, Vicars Lane, Chester CH1 1QX (01244 402111, Fax 01244 403188).
**Nantwich** Church House, Church Walk, Nantwich, Cheshire CW5 5RG (01270 610983, Fax 01270 610880, email: tourist@netcentral.co.uk).
**Market Drayton** 49 Cheshire Street, Market Drayton, Shropshire TF9 1PH, (01630 652139, email: marketdrayton. tourism@shropshire-cc.gov.uk). Also visit www.virtual-shropshire.co.uk.

# Contacts

Ellesmere Port 22b Cheshire Oaks Outlet Village, Kinsey Road, Ellesmere Port, Cheshire CH65 9JJ (0151 356 7879, www.ellesmereport-neston.gov.uk).

## Canal Societies

**Inland Waterways Association**, PO Box 114, Rickmansworth, Hertfordshire WD3 1ZY (01923 711114, Fax 01923 897000; email: iwa@waterways.org.uk, www waterways.org.uk/index.htm).

**Shropshire Union Canal Society**, 4 Eaton Court, Exeter Road, Teignmouth, Devon TQ14 9LZ (01626 777951, www.shropshireunion.co.uk).

**Shrewsbury & Newport Canals Trust**, 4 Arscott, Pontesbury, Shrewsbury SY5 0XP (01743 860488, www.sncanal.org.uk).

## Hire Boat Companies on the Shropshire Union Canal

**Association of Pleasure Craft Operators**, Parkland House, Audley Avenue, Newport, Shropshire TF10 7BX (01952 813572, Fax 01952 820363; email: apco@britishmarine.co.uk, www.britishmarine.co.uk). This is the trade association for hire and hotel boat operators.

**Andersen Boats**, Wych House Lane, Middlewich, Cheshire CW10 9BQ (01606 833668, Fax 01606 837767, www.andersenboats.com).

**Anglo-Welsh Waterway Holidays**, Anglo-Welsh Waterway Holidays, 2 The Hide Market, West Street, St Philips, Bristol B52 0BH (0117 304 1122, Fax 0117 304 1133, www.anglowelsh.co.uk).

**Chas Hardern (Boats) & Co**, Beeston Castle Wharf, Beeston, Tarporley, Cheshire CW6 9NH (01829 732595, Fax 01829 730395, www.chashardern.co.uk).

**Countrywide Cruisers**, The Wharf, Brewood, Staffordshire ST19 9BG (01902 850166, Fax 01902 851662, www.countrywide-cruisers.com).

**Empress Holidays**, Basin End, Nantwich, Cheshire CW5 8LA (01270 624075, Fax 01270 610274, www.empressholidays.com).

**Middlewich Narrowboats**, Canal Terrace, Middlewich, Cheshire CW10 9BD (01606 832460, Fax 01606 737912, www.middlewichboats.co.uk).

**Water Travel**, Autherley Junction, Oxley Moor Road, Wolverhampton WV9 5HW (01902 782371, Fax 01902 787374, wwwwater-travel.co.uk).

## Hotel Boats

Among the hotel boat operators that include the Shropshire Union Canal in their itineraries are:

**Inland Waterway Holiday Cruises**, Greenham Lock Cottage, London Road, Newbury, Berkshire RG14 5SN (07831 110811).

## Public Transport

### Buses

National Express (nationwide service) (08705 808080, www.nationalexpress.com). The national traveline (0870 6082608) will provide rail or coach information nationally and local bus information.

### Trains

Times and fares are best obtained from the National Enquiry Number (08475 484950) or www.nationalrail.co.uk. Stations at Ellesmere Port, Chester and Nantwich are within easy reach of the canal; that at Wolverhampton will require a taxi or bus ride from Autherley.

## The Ellesmere Canal Wirral Line

*The northernmost length of the Shropshire Union Canal main line, which we now think of as a unified whole, was built as the Ellesmere Canal's Wirral Line.*

### Ellesmere Port

*All services, Early Closing Wed, Market Days Tue, Fri, Sat. Tourist Info is out of town at Cheshire Oaks Outlet Village (0151 356 7879, www.ellesmereport-neston.gov.uk).*

Two hundred years ago the industrial town that we call Ellesmere Port was a tiny village on the banks of the river Mersey known as Netherpool. Not until the completion of the network of canals linking south Merseyside with Ellesmere in Shropshire did the name Ellesmere Port become established. Approaching

from the south, as all boaters are likely to do unless they make the difficult and bureaucratically complicated passage of the Manchester Ship Canal (but see below), Ellesmere Port comes as an exciting finale to the Shropshire Union Canal's long haul from the West Midlands. Suddenly, as you pass under the final bridge leading to the port complex, the great Mersey estuary lies ahead of you: an invigorating view whatever the weather. The wind here is certainly always invigorating and it pays to remember that the expression boatmen used for turning their horse boats round is derived from the fact that long light craft will turn themselves if you let the wind help.

Crouched between the Mersey and the Shropshire Union is the Manchester Ship Canal. Opened throughout in 1894, it is sadly less busy now than in the past but there's still enough shipping to attract

**The ultimate British canal passes immediately alongside the Boat Museum at Ellesmere Port. Inland boaters must comply with the Manchester Ship Canal Company's regulations to make the passage to Hulme Lock at Manchester or to the river Weaver. Many will prefer simply to watch those with larger craft passing by. Vessels like this Stanlow-bound tanker, have assistance from tugs ahead and astern, which aid steering in the restricted channel.**

*Euan Corrie*

the attention of the inland waterway enthusiast. Ellesmere Port was once a thriving trans-shipment port where sea-going vessels would transfer cargoes from and to barges and narrowboats. Nowadays we are lucky that parts of the port, and examples of many of the inland waterway vessels which formerly used it, form 'The Boat Museum'.

Ellesmere Port itself is an extremely good shopping centre; a point to replenish the galley before the journey home. The multiple stores seem much better stocked than their counterparts further south, and the bustling covered market is a good spot for a bargain. Pubs and restaurants, though, are thin on the ground. The *Holiday Inn* prominent in the view from the museum, is built on the foundations of a magnificent warehouse designed by Thomas Telford which was destroyed by fire in the 1970s. It offers food and bars as well as accommodation. By the bottom basin is the *Grosvenor*, a more traditional dock gate

hotel and between the museum buildings and the motorway is the *Horse & Jockey* (Banks). Near to the dock complex under the flyover by the bottom basin, is a useful general store open until 9pm every day. On the way up the main road into town you pass B&Q's DIY superstore, Kwik Save, a café, a camping shop selling Gaz and a garage. There are local trains to Rock Ferry (Birkenhead) and Helsby (for Manchester, etc). Bus services connect Ellesmere Port with Chester and Merseyside.

## The Boat Museum

South Pier Road, Ellesmere Port, Cheshire CH65 4FW. (051 355 5017, www. boatmuseum.org.uk). Situated in the historic dock complex at the junction of the Shropshire Union and Manchester Ship canals the Museum is open throughout the year, daily during the summer but closed on Thursday and Friday in winter. There is something for all the family at this working museum of canals, canal boats

*Euan Corrie*

**The Boat Museum hosts a spectacular gathering of privately preserved working narrowboats over the Easter Weekend but its unique collection of all shapes and sizes of trading and maintenance craft which can be visited at any time of year is of national importance.**

# MAP 1
## Ellesmere Port to Bridge 135A

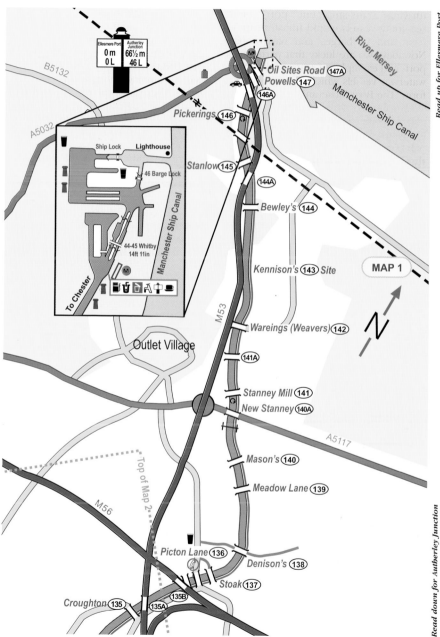

| Ellesmere Port | Autherley Junction |
|---|---|
| 0 m | 66½ m |
| 0 L | 46 L |

River Mersey

Oil Sites Road (147A)
Powells (147)
(146A)
Pickerings (146)
Manchester Ship Canal

Ship Lock    Lighthouse
46 Barge Lock
Stanlow (145)
(144A)
Bewley's (144)
44-45 Whitby
14ft 11in

Manchester Ship Canal

Kennison's (143) Site

MAP 1

To Chester

Wareings (Weavers) (142)

N

Outlet Village
(141A)

M53

Stanney Mill (141)
New Stanney (140A)

A5117

Mason's (140)

Meadow Lane (139)

Top of Map 2

M56

Picton Lane (136)
Denison's (138)
Stoak (137)
Croughton (135)  (135A)  (135B)

B5132

A5032

and barges. First opened in 1976, the Museum will transport you back to the life and times of the canals a century and more ago. There is a large indoor exhibition of canal history and over 40 preserved narrow boats and barges – ranging from the former Thomas Clayton tar boat *Gifford* and the canal tunnel tug *Worcester*, to the Mersey Flat *Mossdale* and the former ICI 300-ton motor barge *Cuddington* – all of which have been preserved by the Museum. There are also restored steam pumping engines, a power hall, where internal combustion engines large and small can be seen running, a café, a shop and a trip boat.

In 1984 The Tom Rolt Education and Conference Centre was officially opened by Sonia Rolt widow of L.T.C. Rolt, author of *Narrow Boat* and one of the founders of the Inland Waterways Association. This building also houses the Museum's extensive archive. More boats and additional exhibits are being added to the Museum's collection each year. A visit makes an ideal day out in the north-west. By road the Museum is adjacent to Junction 9 of M53 and there are frequent bus services from Chester and Birkenhead.

---

**Manchester Ship Canal**

Pleasure craft may be taken onto the MSC if they comply with the MSCCo's regulations. They will also need to pay a toll depending on the length of their journey along the Ship Canal. For further details contact The Harbour Master (see Useful Addresses page 11).

---

## Bridges 147–140

The canal leaves the Boat Museum's basins beneath the attractively named Oil Sites Road and motorway link roads, which were the subject of much strife in the 1960s when the MSCCo sought to landscape the historic dock estate into a container terminal and viewed the planned motorway as an ideal barrier to exclude pleasure craft from their waters.

The eventual compromise was the 11ft wide bridges, which exclude original Shropshire Union craft from their rightful waterway to Nantwich. Schemes for removal of the bottle-neck are proposed from time to time. The canal traverses the industrial outskirts of Ellesmere Port; varied and pungent are the aromas! The vast Stanlow oil refineries lie to the east. By mooring between bridges 140 and 141 those with excess cash or flexible plastic would be able to walk under the motorway to Cheshire Oaks Outlet Village where they can be relieved of any surplus at various designer outlets. The Blue Planet Aquarium (0906 941 0088, www. blueplanetaquarium.com) is nearby if you need to break away from canal water to Scottish glens or Caribbean sharks and their aquatic life; as is the Tourist Information Centre (0151 356 7879).

## Stoak ❚ ⓒ

The M56 and M53 extensions cut across the canal – too close for comfort, one suspects, for the tiny village of Stoak, where the *Bunbury Arms* serves good inexpensive bar meals Mon–Fri lunchtimes and draught Guinness.

## Bridges 135–131

Permanent moorings are sometimes available near Bridge 135. The canal dreams itself along a reedy length between low-lying fields. Chester, indeed all civilisation, seems far away. Chester Zoo (01244 380280, www.chesterzoo.org.uk) one of the largest in Europe, and one where the animals enjoy at least a token amount of freedom, is only half a mile up the lane from the pretty iron-arched Caughall Bridge (134). The Zoo and gardens are open daily from 10am until dusk.

## Bridge 131A

Carrying the Chester–Birkenhead railway, this impressive viaduct dates from 1839. This was once the Birkenhead Joint Railway owned by the London & North Western and Great Western railways and

## MAP 2
### Bridges 135 to 129

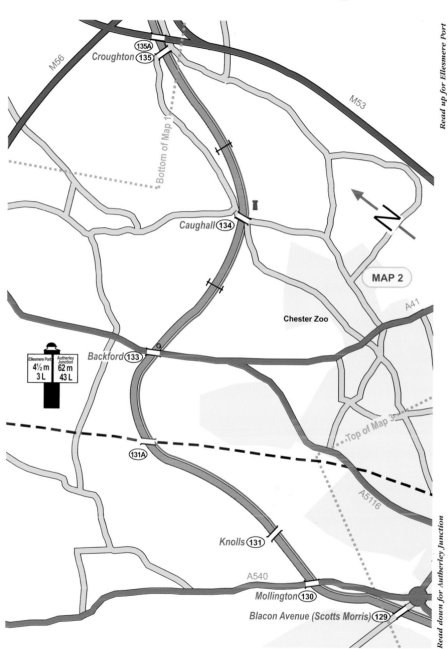

Read up for Ellesmere Port

M56

Croughton 135A
135

Bottom of Map 1

Caughall 134

MAP 2

N

Chester Zoo

M53

A41

| Ellesmere Port | Autherley Junction |
| --- | --- |
| 4½ m | 62 m |
| 3 L | 43 L |

Backford 133

Top of Map 3

131A

A5116

Knolls 131

A540

Mollington 130

Blacon Avenue (Scotts Morris) 129

Read down for Autherley Junction

forming part of the latter's main line from Paddington to Birkenhead Woodside. Until the coming of the railway, the canal company ran a regular horse-drawn service of passenger packets between Chester and Ellesmere Port, where the passengers could transfer into another vessel for the voyage on to Liverpool.

## Bridges 129–128

Modern housing encroaches on the canal as it runs through the northern outskirts of Chester, crossing the modern Deva Link Aqueduct over the ring road, but there are still good views westwards towards the hills of Wales. The floodlit stadium is home for Chester FC.

## The Chester Canal

*The Chester Canal ascended originally directly from the Dee through a flight of locks of which the present Northgate staircase formed the top three chambers. With the construction of the Ellesmere Canal's Wirral line a junction was formed at Tower Wharf and the lower part of the original route to the Dee was re-aligned.*

Standing at the top of Northgate Locks it is possible to appreciate how the staircase points directly at the surviving bottom lock on the river bank. Those boating southwards must nowadays make a sharp left turn to join the older Chester Canal and continue towards Nantwich.

## Tower Wharf ▬ 🛆 👤 🖫 🍴

The canal opens out into a sizeable basin, which is really the most pleasant place to moor for a stay in Chester. The water point is beside the covered drydock (which can be hired by 'phoning BW) whilst the sanitary station is next to the top lock of the Dee Branch. On the other side of the canal

*Euan Corrie*

**British Waterways' 'heritage boats'** *Lindsay* **and** *Keppel* **pass the extensive slipways that form part of the former Shropshire Union Dockyard at Chester. The largest surviving boatyard on the canal system which is subject to repeated proposals for redevelopment as opposed to schemes to keep it in use for its original purpose.**

# MAP 3
## Bridges 129 to 121

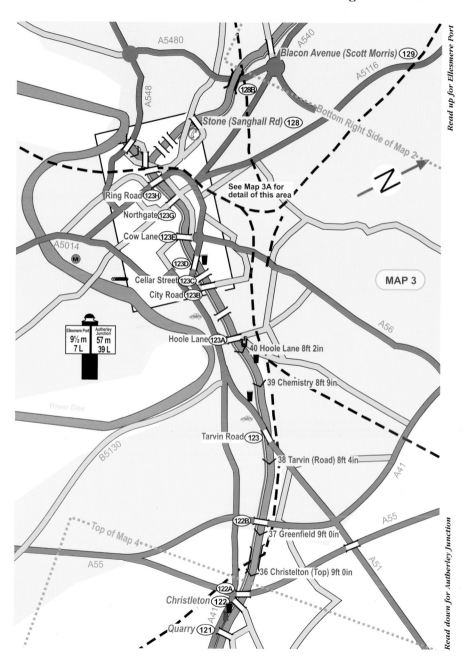

A5480

A540

A5116

Blacon Avenue (Scott Morris) 129

Read up for Ellesmere Port

A548

128B

Bottom Right Side of Map 2

Stone (Sanghall Rd) 128

See Map 3A for detail of this area

N

Ring Road 123H

MAP 3

Northgate 123G

Cow Lane 123E

A5014

M

123D

Cellar Street 123C

City Road 123B

A56

| Ellesmere Port | Autherley Junction |
|---|---|
| 9½ m | 57 m |
| 7 L | 39 L |

Hoole Lane 123A

40 Hoole Lane 8ft 2in

39 Chemistry 8ft 9in

River Dee

B5130

Tarvin Road 123

38 Tarvin (Road) 8ft 4in

A41

Top of Map 4

122B

37 Greenfield 9ft 0in

A55

A55

A51

36 Christelton (Top) 9ft 0in

122A

Christleton 122

A41

Read down for Autherley Junction

Quarry 121

some of the handsome old wharf buildings survive. One now houses a pub/wine bar – *Telford's Warehouse,* which serves lunches and evening meals every day and offers panoramic views over the basin.

A short walk uphill from the corner of the North Basin, turning left at the top of the street, will bring you to local shops, takeaway and launderette.

**David Jones** (01244 376363) ⬤ occupies much of the former Taylors' Dockyard, which was built to service the Shropshire Union Railway & Canal Co's extensive carrying fleet. He specializes in wooden boat repairs and restoration.

## Chester

*All services. Tourist Info: Town Hall, Northgate Street (01244 402111, www. chestertourism.com).*

From the moorings at Tower Wharf the city may be reached by two attractive walks, one leads through the wicket gate from the towpath between the basin and Dee Branch, across Raymond Street/South View Road and up steps to the city wall ahead. Once on the walls you could turn left and follow the canal to descend into Northgate Street or right and pass above the playing fields to reach Watergate Street. If you wish to keep to familiar ground follow the towing path up Northgate Locks and under the inner ring road, in a few yards you can climb to Water Tower Street which leads along the inside of the walls to Northgate Street and the shops. If you're moored in noisier surroundings by Cow Lane Bridge, the centre is only minutes away down Frodsham Street which leads passed modern and more traditional pubs, Marks & Spencer, Tesco and various banks.

This lovely old city with a crowded past has its feet placed firmly in the present day realms of commerce. It's the sort of place for which you don't really need a guidebook – just stroll along its marvelous streets at your own pace. The city wall, which has kept aggressors out down the ages, has also prevented the city from

spreading. Chester is the only English city with its walls more or less intact: a complete circuit is a two-mile walk. It's a walk through the history books past Roman remains, the site of Chester's river port which thrived during the Middle Ages, the tower where King Charles watched his Cavaliers routed by the Roundheads for the last and decisive time, and more, much more, besides.

Top, though, of anyone's list will obviously be the Cathedral. Dating from 1092 it was formerly a Benidictine Abbey but, of course, it's been much added to, especially by the Victorians. Remember though that it isn't just a monument to architecture, it's a living place of worship – Evensong (sung on Sun 3.30pm, Sat 4.15pm and Tue and Thur 5.15pm) is an especially moving experience.

One of Chester's most remarkable features is 'The Rows', which are first floor balconies above street level shops. The reason for their medieval origin remains a mystery, but they offer today's shopper something unique. Half way down 'The Rows' on the east side of Bridge Street is St Michael's Arcade, the handsome Victorian equivalent of the modern Grosvenor shopping precinct to which it, in turn, leads. Eastgate Street is the city's principal thoroughfare. The huge clock above the gate itself commemorates Queen Victoria's Diamond Jubilee. Eastgate has plenty of typical Cheshire 'black & white' buildings, together with some particularly fine examples of early neo-classical and florid counterpoint in styles. Museums are thick on the ground. Chester Visitor Centre (01244 351609) Vicar's Lane (open daily 9.30am–5pm, 10am–4pm on Sundays and longer in summer, admission free) has all the usual tourist office services as well as displays dealing with 2,000 years of Chester's history. The Grosvenor Museum (01244 402008, www.chestercc.gov.uk/heritage/ museum/home) Grosvenor Street (open weekdays 10.30am–5pm, Sun 1–4pm admission free) concentrates on Roman

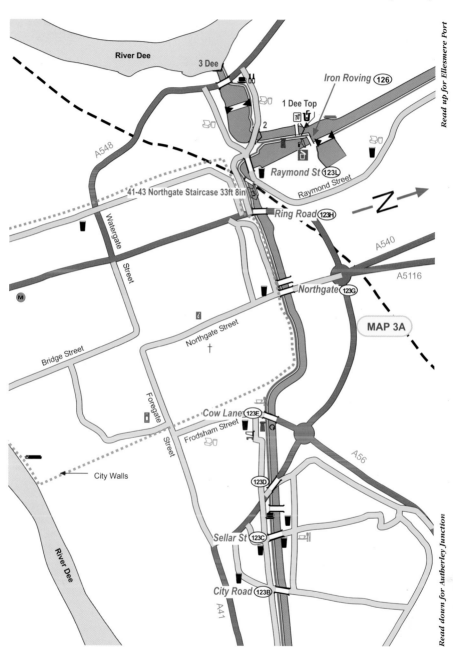

River Dee

3 Dee

Iron Roving (126)

1 Dee Top

2

Raymond St (123L)

Raymond Street

A548

41-43 Northgate Staircase 33ft 8in

Watergate

Ring Road (123H)

-N→

A540

A5116

(M)

Northgate (123G)

MAP 3A

Street

Northgate Street

†

Bridge Street

Cow Lane (123E)

Foregate

Frodsham Street

Street

123D

A56

City Walls

123C Sellar St

River Dee

City Road (123B)

A41

Euan Corrie

**Chester's city centre is well worth a visit – explore the ancient 'rows' where shops are ranged on two levels.**

of restaurants and pubs is almost inexhaustible, the *Albion* in Park Street is a Pubmaster house with Great War Memorabilia, substantial sandwiches and hot meals as well as Timothy Taylor and guest real ales but without machines or music; by the canal at bridge 123C is the *Old Harkers Arms* with real ales, whiskies and meals. Almost opposite is the *Mill Hotel* (01244 350035, www.millhotel. com), which offers full hotel services and good food in a restaurant overlooking the canal, as well as regularly changing real ales. It also operates a restaurant boat which is available for charter by parties, and pre-booked meals on public cruises. The *Union Vaults* at the junction of Egerton and Francis streets is recommended by both the *Good Beer Guide* and *The Good Pub Guide* for its ales. In Eastgate Row try The 17th century *Boot* for a pint of Sam Smiths or a bar meal. As a shopping centre Chester has few rivals outside London. The covered market is open daily except for Wed and Sun: it's behind the Town Hall. For further information on what Chester has to offer the main Tourist Information Centre is next door to the Town Hall in Northgate Street. Conducted walking tours lasting $1\frac{1}{2}$ hours depart from here. A useful booklet called *What's On In Chester* is published monthly free of charge. The city has two cinemas, the Odeon (01244 324930) in Northgate Street and Cannon (01244 322931) in Foregate Street. The Gateway Theatre (01244 340393) in Hamilton Place is one of the leading 'Reps' in the North. For

Chester and local natural history; Chester Military Museum is housed in the Castle (open daily, nominal admission charge). Chester History & Heritage (01244 402110) St Michael's Church, Bridge Street Row www.chestercc.gov.uk/ heritage/history/html) (10am–4pm Mon–Thur, admission charge) illustrates the architectural history of the city and is a useful resource for genealogists. In Chester, gourmets should be prepared to loosen their belts. Worthy of special mention are: the *Romano Hotel* (01244 320841), which is in Lower Bridge Street; *The Witches Kitchen* (01244 311836) Frodsham Street usefully close to the canal by Cow Lane Bridge, a wide choice and open all day long; the *Slow Boat* Chinese restaurant above the freezer centre adjacent to Cow Lane Bridge. The list more strenuous entertainment, the huge Northgate Arena (near the bus station) is open to public for swimming, badminton, table tennis, squash, etc. Chester has comprehensive rail and bus services (see Useful Addresses page 11).

## Northgate Staircase Locks

Harvest House, the old headquarters of the Shropshire Union Canal Company, smiles benignly down on you as you work up or down the huge and heavy-gated Northgate Locks. Those who have not previously encountered staircase locks are referred to the description on page 7.

## Northgate Locks – Bridge 123E

Moat like, the canal follows the foot of Chester's wall. Noisy and limited overnight moorings can be found just north of Cow Lane Bridge (123E) but they have good access via Frodsham Street to the city centre and just up the steps at street level there's a little pub called the *Oddfellows Arms,* which does snacks at lunchtime and Greenall Whitley beers, whilst just along the street on the same side there's a popular fish bar and takeaway. It may also be possible to moor just south of the top lock, but the canal is really too narrow for mooring between these points, and anyone in search of more pleasant and peaceful surroundings or contemplating an extended stop-over in the city should head for Tower Wharf.

## Bridges 123E–122

The canal enters and leaves Chester through surprisingly industrial suburbs. Little 'Coronation Streets' back onto the 'cut' – it could be Burnley or Blackburn and not the Chester of the guidebooks. The *Lock Vaults* by Hoole Lane Lock is a snug pub which offers Tetleys and big screen TV sports. 'Phone and post boxes are nearby and just along Hoole Lane is a useful grocer/newsagent. However, below Tarvin Road Lock, the *Bridge Inn* has mooring bollards outside and offers Whitbread ales, good food and a warm welcome for boaters. The lock may be a good spot for more out of town mooring. A garage with convenience store is handy, fishing tackle across the road and DIY superstore over the canal.

**Narrowboats *Squire* and *Phoebe* descend the three-rise staircase locks at Northgate below Chester's City Walls.**

## The River Dee

For canal travelers it's frustrating that the Dee, navigable for 12 miles from Chester up to Farndon cannot be more easily entered from the canal. As it is, boaters must give at least 48 hours notice to the British Waterways' Office at Northwich (01606 723800) before they can negotiate the Dee Branch with its three locks. Even then, entry to the Dee can only be made an hour either side of high tide Mon–Fri. Downstream the tidal Dee is a fast flowing and often treacherous waterway; hardly suitable for canal craft. It is the haunt of the Dee salmon fishermen who hand their fishing rights down from generation to generation.

Upstream, although the river is more placid, a weir must be crossed at the top of the tide and a licence obtained from the City Council (01244 324324, citycouncil@chestercc.gov.uk) before the upper reaches can be explored. If you really fancy a look at the Dee, then much the easiest way is to hire a boat from Chester Boat Hire or Bithell Boats on The Groves, or take a trip on one of the fine old launches or modern passenger boats which ply up and down to Eccleston Ferry three miles upriver.

Also on The Groves, off Bee Lane, is *The Boathouse* which is open all day, everyday and serves food throughout until 7pm in summer (5pm in winter) as well as Greene King, Bombardier and guest beers all of which may be enjoyed in what it calls 'an all-weather heated covered garden'. Whether it's a deck, terrace or garden, it's an excellent spot to enjoy the river!

**Chester Boat Hire** (01244 400594, www. chesterboathire.co.uk) on The Groves, rowing boat, paddle boat or small motor launches or modern passenger boats.

**Bithells Boats Ltd**, Souters Lane, The Groves, Chester, CH1 1SD (01244 325394, Fax 01244 325396, www. showboatsofchester. co.uk).

*N Christopher*

Experienced boat crews, having made arrangements with British Waterways and Chester City Council, can pass over the weir and enjoy the attractions of the river Dee so long as they remember that time and tide wait for no man. There is a gate in the weir, awkwardly positioned in the corner by the bridge, at the point where the narrowboat is crossing, but it is almost covered by the tide in this view.

*Euan Corrie*

A navigation hazard is created at Tower Wharf at Chester on the Thursday before Easter when working boats heading for Ellesmere Port pause at the normally peaceful moorings. But there is usually a gap for the traffic to pass through.

*Euan Corrie*

Those intent on passing through the Chester Canal's wide locks with two ex-GUCCCo working boats will find the chambers are a little shorter than those the boats were built for and extra care is needed. On 5th April 1999 Fred Heritage watches carefully as the bottom gates of Beeston Stone Lock threaten the immaculate paintwork of *Atlas*. If your boat is 70ft, or less, you will have no such worries.

### Christleton ▬ ▮ ⌐ 🅾 🄲

*Ye Old Trooper* (adjacent to bridge 122) is a Beefeater Steak House offering a combination of bars and restaurants with drinks and meals to suit all tastes, not to mention the Sunday magician! The straggling village becomes prettier nearer its centre. There's a PO/stores and the *Ring o' Bells* with Worthington, Boddingtons, Caffreys and guest ales serving meals at lunchtime and early evenings. Past the pretty church and round a bend is a picturesque duck pond. The old canalside mill has been turned into flats.

Just north of bridge 120 the *Cheshire Cat* is a large Vintage Inn with moorings outside. It has accommodation, Bass and other guest beers, ciders and serves food all day every day.

### K. Farebrother (01244 332633) 🅰 ▮

*slipway, boat and outboard motor repairs and servicing.* By Bridge 120.

### Egg Bridge ⌐ 🄳 🄲

There's a row of shops including a general store, butcher, fashion shop, newsagent and a fruiterer in Waverton about a ¼ mile from the canal. A similar distance to the west is a post office/grocery store open until 9.30pm every day. Waverton Mill has been converted into flats.

### Bridges 118–113

Flat open countryside borders the canal, with the 'pyramid-like' spire of Waverton Church to the west and, in the far distance, the outline of the Welsh hills.

# MAP 4
## Christleton to Bridge 116

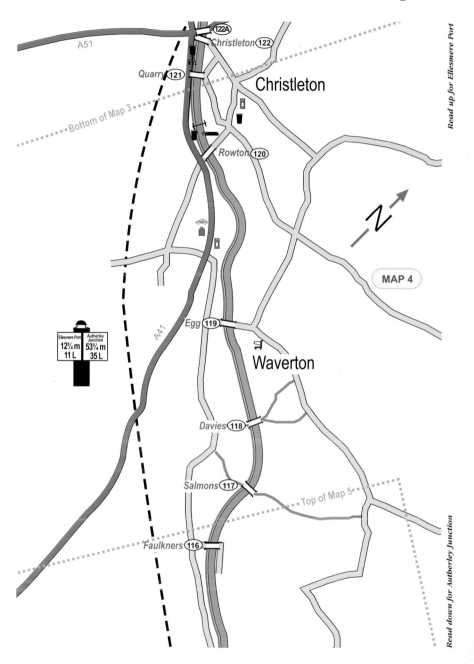

A51

Christleton 122A

Christleton 122

Quarry 121

Christleton

Bottom of Map 3

Rowton 120

MAP 4

A41

Ellesmere Port | Autherley Junction
12¾ m | 53¾ m
11 L | 35 L

Egg 119

Waverton

Davies 118

Salmons 117

Top of Map 5

Faulkners 116

A long length of permanent moorings leads towards the former brick and tile works at Crow's Nest Bridge (113) where there are casual moorings. The Oak Room, a short walk beyond the railway, serves locally brewed Weetwoods beers as well as a good selection of wines and bar and restaurant meals 7 days a week. It also boasts a playground and craft and gift shop with a wide range of stock including candles and mustards.

**Crow's Nest Boat Services** Just south of Bridge 113 (07971 342480) ⬛ 🅰 🔟 🅱 ⬛ 🔋 🍴 *solid fuels, engine and boat repairs (including breakdowns) and servicing. Independent Boat Safety Scheme inspections can be arranged..*

## Bridges 112–111

A pretty tree clothed reverse curve carries the canal over the little river Gowy which eventually finds its way out into the Mersey at Stanlow after being piped under the Manchester Ship Canal.

**Beeston Castle** perched astride its rocky sandstone outcrop 300ft above the Cheshire Plain dominates the landscape hereabouts. It must have appeared an awesome and impregnable fortress to wouldbe attackers! In fact, it suffered a chequered history – dating from the 13th century, ruined by the 16th, but used again during the Civil War. It's open to the public every afternoon, and the best approach for boaters is from Bate's Mill

*English Heritage*

Beeston Castle.

# MAP 5
## Bridge 116 the Gowy Aqueduct

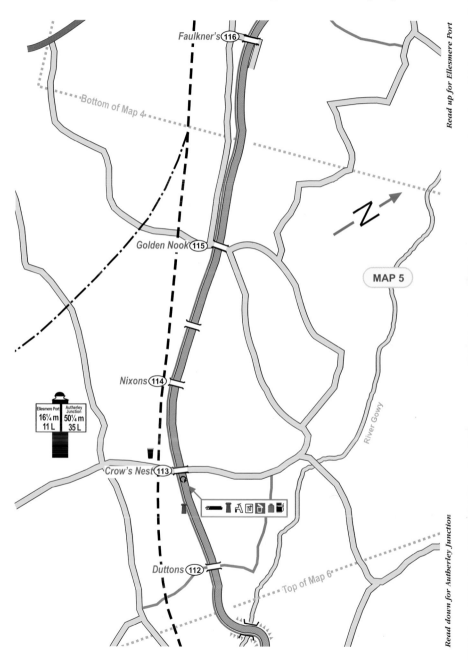

Read up for Ellesmere Port

Faulkner's 116

Bottom of Map 4

Golden Nook 115

MAP 5

Nixons 114

| Ellesmere Port | Autherley Junction |
| --- | --- |
| 16¼ m | 50¼ m |
| 11 L | 35 L |

River Gowy

Crow's Nest 113

Duttons 112

Top of Map 6

Read down for Autherley Junction

Bridge (109) taking the left turn at the T junction, and walking for another ½ mile to the impressive entrance gate. The turreted towers of Peckforton Castle lie on a ridge further to the south. But this castle has never been fought over. It's pure Victorian sham, a home for the first Lord Tollemache. Allow 3 hours for a visit to the castle, and then refresh yourselves at the *Shady Oak* a sophisticated canalside inn, which does John Smiths, Theakstons and Ruddles beers, and bar meals all day, every day. There's a payphone, children are welcome in the garden and conservatory and moorings are available for patrons.

## Wharton's Lock

Cheshire County Council's increasingly popular 'Sandstone Trail', a 34-mile footpath following the central Cheshire ridge from Frodsham in the north to Whitchurch on the Shropshire border, crosses the canal. A very good descriptive leaflet of the trail, which also crosses the Llangollen Canal, is available from all local Tourist Information Centres.

**Emerging from the iron chamber of the the lower lock at Beeston. Broken tie rods underground have caused the chamber to twist, which can cause boats to jam, so take care.**

## Beeston

On Wednesdays and Fridays the cattle market is held up the lane behind the *Beeston Castle Hotel*. Pigs, sheep and cattle are the usual stock in trade but once a month there's a pony sale and from time to time an antique auction too. The *Beeston Castle* is open all day and serves meals (all day on Sunday otherwise every lunch and evening) with real ales draught Guinness and cider and has accommodation. The Lock Gate Café (Bridge 107) is handy for gigantic fry-ups!

**Chas Hardern** (01829 732595) — *solid fuels, hire craft, Boat Safety Scheme inspections, repairs and servicing, fitting out, chandlery.* The family has been taking a personal interest in the customers and individually cherished boats since 1971. Up the outside staircase is Mrs Hardern's 'Glory Hole', an amazing shop with lots of fluffy toys that the children will love – canalia, souvenirs and books for grown-ups too.

## Beeston Locks

The chamber of the lower of the two locks is made, unusually, out of iron. The canal builders took this step to combat quicksand at the base of the lock, earlier brick-built locks having continually suffered from subsidence. Nevertheless, the iron sides have bowed somewhat over the years following breakage of underground tie rods and boaters are recommended not to try fitting two boats over 60ft long side by side in this lock. Shorter boats should not have any trouble when passing through together if they keep a little towards the upper end of the chamber. There's a lovely line of sandy turf-topped hillocks by the locks, and note the circular lock hut, one of three surviving from Chester Canal Co days.

**Tilstone Lock** is picturesquely situated by a former water mill at the foot of a shallow wooded valley.

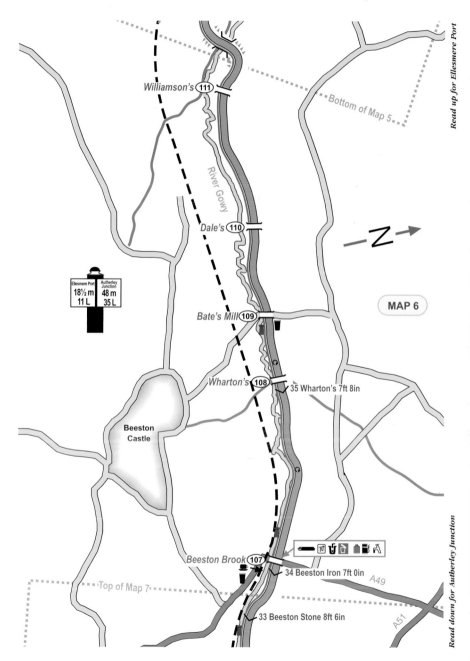

MAP 6
The Gowy to Beeston

Read up for Ellesmere Port

Williamson's (111)

Bottom of Map 5

River Gowy

Dale's (110)

N→

Ellesmere Port 18½ m 11 L
Autherley Junction 48 m 35 L

Bate's Mill (109)

MAP 6

Wharton's (108)

35 Wharton's 7ft 8in

Beeston Castle

Beeston Brook (107)

34 Beeston Iron 7ft 0in

A49

Top of Map 7

33 Beeston Stone 8ft 6in

A51

Read down for Autherley Junction

Etan Corrie

**A narrowboat leaves the bottom of the two rise staircase locks at Bunbury. The fine boat horse stables alongside the top lock occupying the background are used for boat building.**

## Bunbury

The village with its fine church, black and white cottages, and restored water mill (open Sun and Bank Hols afternoons in summer (01829 261422 or www.bunbury-mill.org for details) is a mile to the south-west. In the village, the *Dysart Arms* (01829 260183) is a free house picturesquely situated opposite the church and serving Boddingtons and Timothy Taylors whilst offering food every lunch and early eve. Bunbury was a canal centre in days past when stables beside the staircase locks saw a constant procession of horse-drawn working boats passing through. Today it's a canal centre of a different sort, for the stables have been converted into workshops. The staircase locks have a fall or rise of 15ft 7in (see page 7 if you're unsure as to their operation).

**Anglo-Welsh Waterway Holidays**
Bunbury Locks (01829 260957) *hire craft, servicing, repairs, breakdowns, boatbuilding. There's also a handy post box.* Anglo-Welsh also operate from Norbury Junction and other bases. Hire craft (including day hire) details are available from 0117 304 1122 and www.anglowelsh.co.uk.

## Calveley

The wharf was an active trans-shipment depot between canal and railway until the 1960s. The *Davenport Arms* (which is closed on Monday evenings) has a wonderful collection of teapots, not to mention beer garden and payphone, but perhaps more importantly does lunchtime and evening meals everyday except Monday lunchtime (01829 260470). It serves local Weetwoods beers and guest ales.

## Bridges 104–101

North Western Farmers' huge modern depot lies beside the canal and includes a useful farmers' shop (01829 260988) with some foods, pet food and endless shackles, ropes and other items that might be used aboard a boat just as easily as on the farm. The futuristic radio telescope is linked with the huge one at Jodrell Bank.

# MAP 7
## Beeston to Wardle

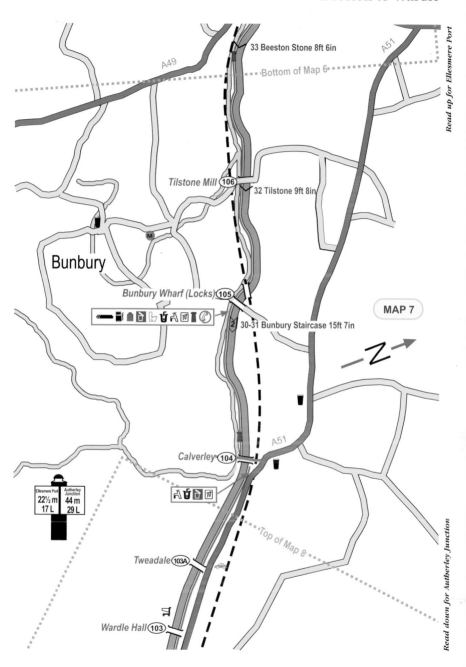

33 Beeston Stone 8ft 6in

A51

A49

Read up for Ellesmere Port

Bottom of Map 6

Tilstone Mill 106

32 Tilstone 9ft 8in

Bunbury

M

Bunbury Wharf (Locks) 105

30-31 Bunbury Staircase 15ft 7in

MAP 7

A51

Calverley 104

| Ellesmere Port | Autherley Junction |
|---|---|
| 22½ m | 44 m |
| 17 L | 29 L |

Top of Map 8

Tweadale 103A

Read down for Autherley Junction

Wardle Hall 103

## Barbridge Junction

This is the junction of the Shropshire Union's Main Line and its Middlewich Branch. Just south of the actual junction (framed by a whitewashed roving bridge) the canal narrows where a covered warehouse used to straddle the channel. The *Jolly Tar Inn* directly opposite the junction is open all day at weekends and has a friendly welcome. It serves Theakstons and good food every lunch and eve, all year. Mooring on either side of the junction is restricted to 48 hrs. The *Barbridge Inn* (01270 528443) by Bridge 100 offers special moorings for patrons, Boddingtons bitter, Bombardier and guests with home cooked food every lunch and evening, summer barbecues, and has a canalside garden and play area.

The ten-mile long Middlewich Branch (see page 64) tends to be undervalued by waterway enthusiasts. Generally regarded as a convenient through route between the 'Shroppie' and the Trent & Mersey Canal, it's a very beautiful canal, well worth including in any itinerary for its own sake. It passes through sparsely populated countryside with big farms whose fields are filled with cows or ploughed like corduroy into the red Cheshire soil.

**Barbridge Marina (Midway Boats Ltd)**
On the Middlewich Branch immediately beyond the roving bridge (01270 528682) *solid fuel, slipway up to 30ft, boat sales and brokerage, chandlery, Boat Safety Scheme inspections, boat and engine repairs and breakdowns, outboard sales and servicing, boat transport.*

## Hurleston Junction

The Welsh Section of the Shropshire Union system, nowadays usually referred to as the Llangollen Canal, climbs away from the Main Line by the Hurleston flight of four locks. Llangollen is 22 hours cruising time away. The *Waterways World Guide to the Llangollen and Montgomery Canals* covers the route in detail.

**This view of an overcrowded Barbridge (Middlewich Branch under the towpath bridge to the left of centre) dates from before 1921 when the Shropshire Union Railways & Canal Co gave up their large carrying fleet, and is thought to have been taken on the occasion of a strike. The warehouse spanned the narrows south of the junction until the mid 20th century. The Canal Inspector's house beyond the bridge still stands.**

Waterway Images

# MAP 8
## Barbridge to Hurleston

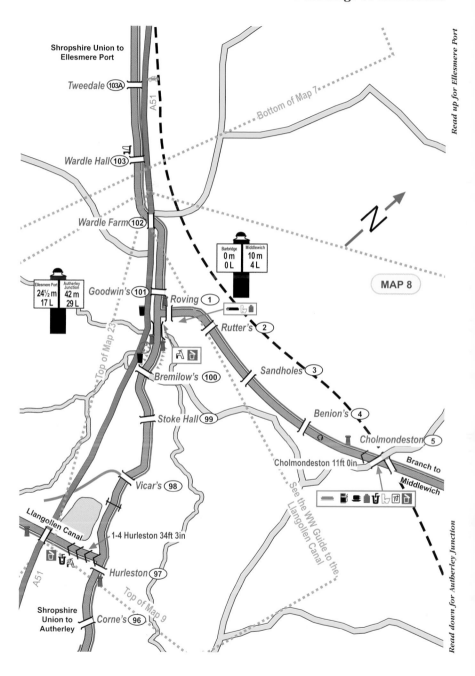

Shropshire Union to
Ellesmere Port

Read up for Ellesmere Port

Tweedale (103A)

A51

Bottom of Map 7

Wardle Hall (103)

N

Wardle Farm (102)

MAP 8

| Barbridge | Middlewich |
|---|---|
| 0 m | 10 m |
| 0 L | 4 L |

| Ellesmere Port | Autherley Junction |
|---|---|
| 24½ m | 42 m |
| 17 L | 29 L |

Goodwin's (101)

Roving (1)

Rutter's (2)

Top of Map 23

Bremilow's (100)

Sandholes (3)

Benion's (4)

Stoke Hall (99)

Cholmondeston (5)

Cholmondeston 11ft 0in

Branch to
Middlewich

See the WW Guide to the
Llangollen Canal

Vicar's (98)

Llangollen Canal

1-4 Hurleston 34ft 3in

A51

Hurleston (97)

Top of Map 9

Shropshire
Union to
Autherley

Corne's (96)

Read down for Autherley Junction

Shropshire Union Canal 35

## Bridges 96–93

The canal works its way through pleasant farmland. The tower of Acton Church can be seen peeping above a line of trees to the west. A 19th century Beadle of the Church used to walk the aisle during services tapping over the head any of the congregation seen falling asleep! *The Star* is a short walk from Bridge 93 and is open all day, every day, with a garden and B&B accommodation. It is a pleasant country pub offering food every lunchtime and evening and Bass or Worthington by the open fire.

## Nantwich Basin End  ▬

The original terminal basin of the Chester Canal is now known as Nantwich Marina and offers a canal shop and facilities. Through travelers not wishing to divert into the basin can take on water from a tap on the off-side between Empress Holidays' boatyard and Bridge 92.

**Nantwich Canal Centre** Basin End, Nantwich (01270 625122)  ▬ ▮ 📅 🔥

🔥 ⛽ 🏠 🛢 ⌂ Ⓒ 🔧 *solid fuels, cranage, Boat Safety Scheme inspections, boat brokerage, building, painting and fitting out, servicing, breakdowns and repairs, (CORGI registered gas fitting), large chandlery, book and gift shop.*

## Bridges 93–91

For boaters, Nantwich is a frontier town. Whether you're cruising northwards or southwards the difference will immediately be apparent. The winding, contour-following, broad waters of the old Chester Canal to the north give way to the straight cuttings and embankments of the narrow Birmingham & Liverpool Junction Canal to the south, or vice versa. The canal appears to deliberately avoid Nantwich on a vast embankment to the west of the town. It crosses the A534 Chester Road on one of Telford's cast iron aqueducts. In fact this diversion was only constructed at the insistence of Mr

Timkinson the owner of Dorfold Hall who feared the desecration of his park which would result from construction of Telford's intended route directly from the end of the Chester Canal basin towards Marsh Lane. The embankment at first refused to stand and has been prone to subsidence ever since. Only in very recent times has any mooring been permitted along it and you are still recommended to use the rings rather than driving spikes into the towpath edge. Mooring on certain sections of the embankment is either prohibited entirely, or restricted to 24 hours. Take care to leave room for full length craft making the turn at the aqueduct.

**Empress Holidays** (01270 624075) 📅
🛢 *hire craft and skippered evening cruises to the* Barbridge Inn, *RYA training courses.*

# The Birmingham & Liverpool Junction Canal

*North of Nantwich the canal route comprises of what was originally the Chester Canal, opened to Nantwich from Chester in 1779 at which time Chester was an important port. It is difficult for us to imagine today that, for over 50 years, the canal stopped at Nantwich. The extension to Autherley Junction was not completed until 1835. Prior to this, the main route to the Midlands was via the Trent & Mersey Canal through the Potteries. From Nantwich to Chester the canal is a broad-locked waterway originally used by barges, known locally as 'flats', off the river Dee southwards the newer B&LJ was built to accommodate only the Midlands' narrowboat.*

## Nantwich

*All services, Early Closing Wed, Market Day Thur (am) & Sat. Tourist Info: Church Walk (01270 610983, tourist@net-central.co.uk).*
A charming old market town, which has

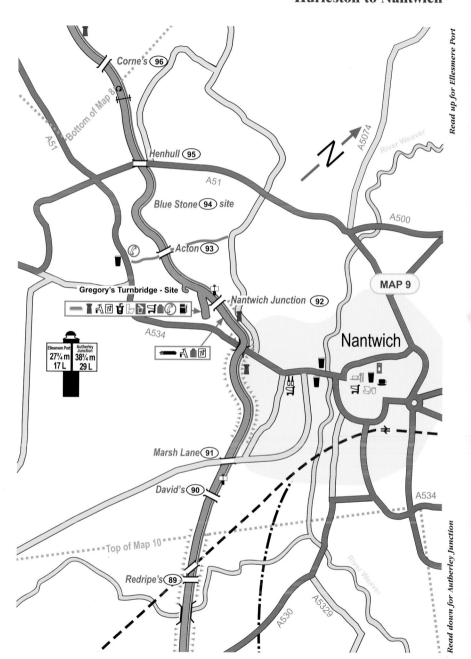

MAP 9
**Hurleston to Nantwich**

Read up for Ellesmere Port

Corne's 96

Bottom of Map 8

A51

Henhull 95

A51

Blue Stone 94 site

River Weaver

A5074

A500

Acton 93

MAP 9

Gregory's Turnbridge - Site

Nantwich Junction 92

Nantwich

A534

| Ellesmere Port | Autherley Junction |
|---|---|
| 27¾ m | 38¾ m |
| 17 L | 29 L |

Marsh Lane 91

David's 90

Top of Map 10

Redripe's 89

River Weaver

A534

A530

A5329

Read down for Autherley Junction

benefited by the provision of an inner ring road taking traffic out of the narrow winding streets of the centre. It's a prosperous place, the shops, pubs and restaurants have a confident well-to-do look about them that adds to the pleasure of a visit. The town centre is 15–20 minutes walk from the canal – turn left outside the basin, or come down the steps off the embankment by the aqueduct. Look about during the walk in to town along Welsh Row, one of the best streets. Along the way one passes the pretty Tollemache almshouses, a convenient general store open until 9pm every day, a popular fish & chip bar, some handsome half-timbered and Georgian houses, and plenty of pubs. The *Black Lion* offers local Weetwoods beers and ciders as well as bar meals and live music at weekends. Superb bar meals are served at the *Oddfellows Arms* (except on Mondays) – we particularly enjoyed the 'Nutty Stilton & Mushroom Pie'! The *Wilbraham Arms* also serves meals and is open all day. A row of half-timbered 17th century widows' almshouses turn out to have been converted into *Curshaws* (01270 623020) which is open all day, from 9.30am, and serves food from breakfast onwards as well as offering accommodation. The *Swan with Two Necks* is an Enterprise Inn, and nearby are *The Indian Ocean* (01270 629928) balti restaurant and takeaway; a southern fried chicken; kebabs; burgers and Chinese food to take away.

A stone bridge over the river Weaver leads into the centre. For newcomers there's a helpful Tourist Information Centre near the Church. It has details of guided tours of the town, or you can purchase an inexpensive little booklet called *Walkabout Tour of Nantwich,* a good introduction to the town. But those who disdain such an organised approach can simply wander about under their own steam, for the town is compactly laid out, one street of delights enticing you on the next. Three 'musts', however, are the 12th century Parish Church of St Mary with its splendid octagonal steeple and its surpris-

ing reference to the pagan tree worshippers; the nearby row of fine Georgian townhouses known as the Dysart Buildings, an example of 18th century speculative building which says little for anything we've done since; and across the lawns opposite the Church the *Crown Hotel,* a symphony in half-timber built in 1585, and workplace of a late 19th century coach driver called 'old Piggott' grandfather of a slightly better known horseman of more recent times. The *Crown* also offers Boddingtons, Flowers and draught Bass, bar meals at lunchtime and restaurant service in the evenings; which specializes in Italian cuisine. It hosts live music and organizes the annual Nantwich Jazz & Blues Festival. *The Vine* in Hospital Street is highly recommended for its interesting nooks and crannies, Bass and Worthington and Sunday Lunches; food is served every lunchtime (except Monday when the pub is closed) and all except Sunday to Tuesday evenings. *The Shakespeare* on Beam Street specializes in Indian food. Churches' Mansion on London Road, was described by L.T.C. Rolt after his visit to its tea shop in 1939 and remains an astonishingly beautiful 400 year-old half-timbered house. It is now an antique shop but worth visiting for its own sake. A small museum devoted to Nantwich's history – much of it to do with the once all-important salt trade – is situated in Pillory Street. Nantwich Railway Station is served by local trains between Crewe and Shrewsbury with good connections at both points.

At **Hack Green** Top Lock the old stables are now used by British Waterways for storing maintenance gear. The moorings between the lock and bridge provide the ideal starting point for the short walk to one of Cheshire's most closely guarded secrets – Hack Green Nuclear Bunker (01270 629219, www.hackgreen.co.uk). This Cold War fall-out shelter and administrative headquarters for north-west England is now open to the public daily 10.30am–5pm in summer and 11am–4.30pm on winter weekends.

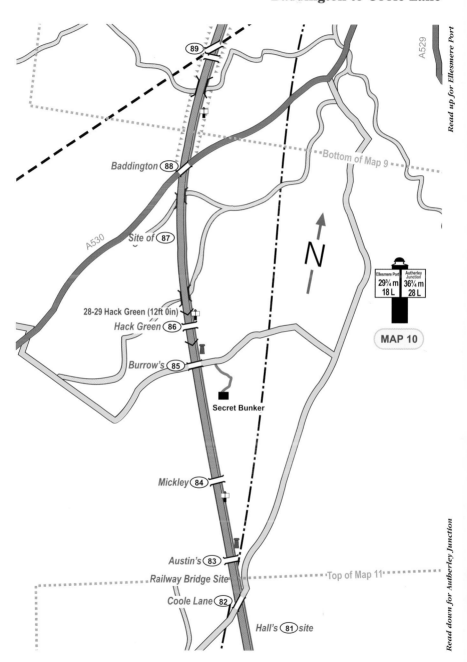

## MAP 10
## Baddington to Coole Lane

Read up for Ellesmere Port

A529

89

Bottom of Map 9

Baddington 88

A530

Site of 87

N

Ellesmere Port 29¾ m 18 L  Autherley Junction 36¾ m 28 L

MAP 10

28-29 Hack Green (12ft 0in)

Hack Green 86

Burrow's 85

Secret Bunker

Mickley 84

Austin's 83

Railway Bridge Site

Top of Map 11

Coole Lane 82

Hall's 81 site

Read down for Autherley Junction

## Bridges 84–80

Black and white cattle fill the fields, for these are the prosperous dairy farms of the Cheshire Plain

## Audlem 🚂🍴🛏 🚮 🅿

*Early Closing Wed.*

Shops and pubs huddle round the Parish Church of St James the Great, at the foot of which lies the village square and the columned buttermarket. The *Lamb Hotel* offers bar meals every lunch & eve and has a restaurant open Mon–Sat lunch and Tue–Sat eve. Children are welcome and there's a garden. Opposite the church is the *Lord Combermere*, a friendly free house serving Theakstons and with bar meals every lunch & on all but Sunday evening with a children's room and play area. *The Old Priest House Coffee Shop* nearby on Stafford Street is open from 10am until dusk for an excellent choice of light meals and refreshments. Williams' Drapers and Newsagents in the square could be mistaken for a miniature department store; it even offers a dry cleaning service. If you cross the playing fields behind the *Shroppie Fly* you'll emerge opposite Audlem's excellent fish & chip shop, open Mon–Sat. John Stothert has converted the erstwhile Kingbur Mill into the marvelous Audlem Mill Canal Shop & Gallery, one of the best on the canals. He stocks a wide selection of souvenirs and books as well as a wide variety of artwork including paintings by Sheila Webster and Harley Crossley among others. Alongside the third lock of the Audlem flight is the *Shroppie Fly Inn* which in summer serves everything from morning coffee to evening meals. Incidentally, the pillar crane outside came from the railway station goods shed just down the road. By Bridge 78 is the *Bridge Inn*, a Marston's house with Pedigree on draught and Owd Roger from the wood in winter. Food is served every lunchtime and evening. Don't miss the puddings!

**J.W. Motors** (01270 811458) 🛢 will deliver Calor Gas to boats at the wharf.

Buses run from Audlem, via Nantwich, to Crewe railway station.

### Audlem Locks 🔧🚽🚮

A flight of 15 locks lowers the canal into or raises it out of Cheshire. The total rise or fall is 93ft. The locks lie partly in a shallow cutting clothed with fir and pine trees. Note the care Thomas Telford took in laying out the Birmingham & Liverpool Junction Canal: the vast majority of the locks are neatly grouped in evenly spaced flights, making horse boating as easy as possible. Furthermore, from Wheaton Aston the fall of each lock is slightly smaller than those of the flight upstream, thus the water sent down should always be sufficient, with a little over, to supply the lock below.

Mooring between Bridge 78 and Lock 13 is restricted to 24 hours, but you can moor on both sides of the canal. Note also that there is water along with Elsan and rubbish disposal facilities near Lock 13.

Fresh produce or flowers are for sale in season beside Lock 9 – leave your money in the box on the fence.

## Windlass in My Belt
### *a canal adolescence*  by John Thorpe

An autobiographical and evocative tale of a young boy's journey into manhood and his acceptance into the canal community of the Midlands and life on a working boat in the 1950s and 60s

Published by Waterways World        **296 pages  pbk  1 870002 96 2  £14.99**

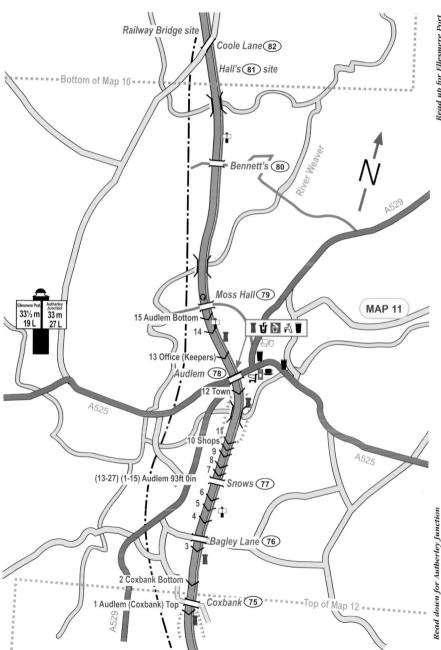

MAP 11
Audlem

Railway Bridge site

Coole Lane 82

Hall's 81 site

Bottom of Map 10

Bennett's 80

River Weaver

A529

N

Read up for Ellesmere Port

Ellesmere Port 33½ m 19 L — Autherley Junction 33 m 27 L

Moss Hall 79

15 Audlem Bottom

14

13 Office (Keepers)

Audlem 78

12 Town

MAP 11

A525

11

10 Shops

9

8

7

Snows 77

(13-27) (1-15) Audlem 93ft 0in

6

5

4

Bagley Lane 76

3

A525

2 Coxbank Bottom

1 Audlem (Coxbank) Top

Coxbank 75

Top of Map 12

A529

Read down for Autherley Junction

*Kevin Maslin*

The Audlem flight is often busy and traffic tends to bunch up because top gate paddles have been removed from some of the locks. If boat crews stick to the 'one up – one down' rule water, time and temper will all be saved as boats will pass through the flight steadily without grounding in unnecessarily emptied pounds.

## Adderley Locks

This lovely flight was well known for many years for its immaculate flower beds and neatly mown grass tended by the lock keeper, Frank Butter. Although Mr Butter died in 1989, the flight retains some of the shrubs and trees he planted and the top of the flight is a delightful place to moor.

## Bridges 68–65

Bridge 67 is a graceful 'roving' bridge carrying the towing path over to the opposite side of the canal. The canal traverses flat, open, farmland, passing through a pretty cutting that is reputedly haunted; perhaps that explains why it is teeming with wildlife! The parapets of an old railway bridge can be seen amidst encroaching vegetation. This former North Stafford Railway line used to carry trains between Market Drayton and Stoke-on-Trent. The earthworks of another abandoned railway, the old Great Western's Wellington–Nantwich route, follow the canal closely to the west.

# MAP 12
## Adderley to Betton Wood

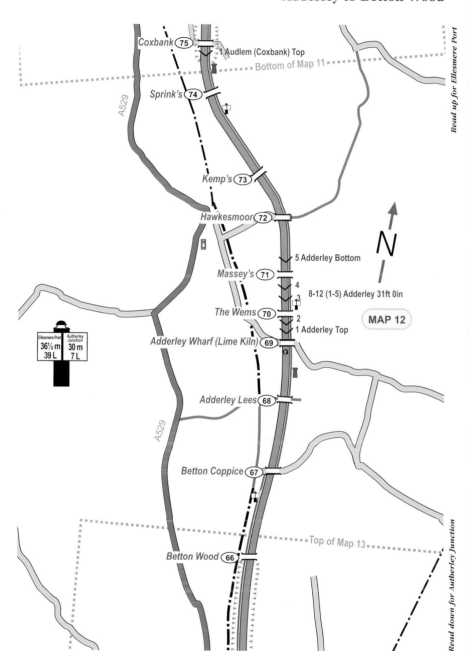

Coxbank (75)

1 Audlem (Coxbank) Top

Bottom of Map 11

Sprink's (74)

A529

Kemp's (73)

Hawkesmoor (72)

5 Adderley Bottom

Massey's (71)

4

8-12 (1-5) Adderley 31ft 0in

3

The Wems (70)

2

1 Adderley Top

Adderley Wharf (Lime Kiln) (69)

MAP 12

Ellesmere Port / Autherley Junction
36½ m / 30 m
39 L / 7 L

Adderley Lees (68)

A529

Betton Coppice (67)

Top of Map 13

Betton Wood (66)

Read up for Ellesmere Port

Read down for Autherley Junction

**Victoria Wharf** Home of H. Orwell coal merchants (01630 652472), those lucky enough to have a solid fuel stove can bunker here.

## Market Drayton

*All services. Market Day Wed. Tourist Info: 49 Cheshire Street (01630 652139, marketdrayton.tourism@shropshire-cc.gov.uk).*

A pleasant, if unspectacular, old town with its fair share of half-timbered buildings which comes to life on Wednesdays when the 700-year old market is held. It begins early, and by 10 o'clock the streets radiating from the Buttercross are a clamouring throng of would-be sellers and buyers. Market Drayton's most famous son, Clive of India, spent his riproaring boyhood in the town; culminating in a legendary ascent of the church tower. The centre is 15 minutes walk from Bridges 62 or 63. The Tourist Office can provide leaflets detailing interesting walks both around the historic parts of the town and in the surrounding countryside.

Talbot Wharf, always a focal point of the canal, and once the site of a British Waterways piling depot where many of the concrete piles protecting the canal originated, remains a hive of activity. There are two boatyards. The fascinatingly shaped Betton Mill houses *Woodies' Canalside Emporium and Tea Room* where a wonderful selection of speciality teas, light refreshments, including ice creams, cream teas and even Sunday lunches may be enjoyed whilst you wait for your model railway equipment to be serviced or repaired! There is also canalia and second hand books and folk music on Thursday evenings.

The *Talbot*, adjacent to Bridge 62, offers vegetarian choices at its lunchtime and evening meals (ex Mon eve) and has a payphone. There are plenty of pubs to choose from: up in the town the *Corbet Arms*, a 17th century coaching inn, which is open all day, offers meals every lunch time and evening as well as afternoon tea. *The Crown* on Stafford Street keeps Marstons beers and offers restaurant and bar meals at lunchtime and evenings – it only closes during the afternoon on a Sunday. *The Stafford Court Hotel* has a restaurant that can offer breakfast to non-residents, from 7.30am and is open all day. After a hot day on the canal the swimming pool is a tantalising 15 minutes walk from the canal.

Buses link with the main line railway stations at Shrewsbury and Stoke-on-Trent.

There is a water point, refuse disposal and pumpout facility on the towpath opposite Talbot Wharf and good visitors moorings south of Bridge 62.

**Ted's Boatyard** in Betton Mill by Bridge 63 (01630 658282) ⚓ Ⓒ 🛢 ❚ 🗲 Ⓐ 𝗵 *(assisted – in contrast to the DIY card-operated machine on the towpath opposite), chandlery, solid fuel, cranage and Boat Safety Scheme inspections by arrangement, boat building, fitting out, painting and repairs, DIY facilities, engine repairs and 24-hour breakdown service, day boat hire and brokerage. Also deals in Lister, Yanmar and Isuzu engines.* Open every day.

**Whisky Boatfitters** (07802 409693) is also in Betton Mill.

**Holidays Afloat** on Talbot Wharf (01630 652937) ⚓ 🛢 ❚ 🗲 *solid fuel, chandlery, boat sales, slipway, engine and boat repairs, fitting out, painting and breakdowns, cranage and Boat Safety Scheme inspections can be arranged. They also build and repair road trailers of all types.* There is a post box at the entrance to the wharf.

**Aquarius Trip Boats** (01630 653719) set off from the towpath north of Bridge 62 at 10.30 and 2pm every Wednesday to Friday in summer with public trips. On Saturdays they operate Candlelit dinner cruises, for which booking is essential. Sunday Lunch cruises travel up Tyrley Locks towards Goldstone, and again booking is essential.

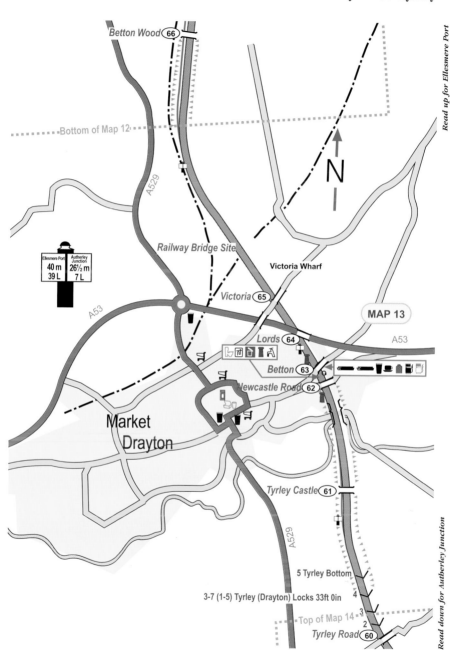

## MAP 13
## Market Drayton to Tyrley

Betton Wood 66

Read up for Ellesmere Port

Bottom of Map 12

N

A529

Railway Bridge Site

| Ellesmere Port | Autherley Junction |
|---|---|
| 40 m | 26½ m |
| 39 L | 7 L |

Victoria Wharf

A53

Victoria 65

MAP 13

A53

Lords 64

Betton 63

Newcastle Road 62

Market Drayton

Tyrley Castle 61

A529

Read down for Autherley Junction

5 Tyrley Bottom

3-7 (1-5) Tyrley (Drayton) Locks 33ft 0in   4

Top of Map 14   3

2

Tyrley Road 60

## Tyrley Locks

Five beautifully situated locks take the canal down into or up out of Market Drayton. Tyrley Cutting, perhaps the darkest and most dripping of 'Shroppie' cuttings, is the haunt of kingfishers, wagtails and bats. Ferns and mosses thrive in the shadowy, damp environment. Towpath walkers will wish they were wearing boots.

**Tyrley Wharf** 🅰 ⛽ 🅱 Dating from 1837, Tyrley Wharf has a picturesque row of Tudor-style cottages built not by the canal company but by the owner of the nearby Peatswood Hall. When you emerge from the top lock, peep round the corner at the memorial to the men of the Peatswood estate who fell in the Great War. Apparently a bunch of poppies appears there mysteriously every Armistice Day. This was once an important overnight mooring place for the Shropshire Union's carrying boats and there was stabling for up to 22 horses. Little sign remains of the stables which stood on the towpath but across the road cars are often parked on the brick floor of the demolished stables by the lock cottage hedge. Half a mile uphill from Bridge 60 is the *Four Alls* (01630 652995) a pub and motel open all day and serving bar and restaurant meals every lunch and evening. Children are welcome.

## Woodseaves Cutting

An astonishing memorial to the men who built the canal. Hewn from solid rock almost by hand, certainly without machinery, this deep cutting extends for over a mile between Bridges 56 and 59. Two high arched overbridges cross it. Woodseaves Cutting was difficult to construct and remains expensive to maintain. Care should be taken when passing oncoming boats.

## Cheswardine 🍴 🍺 🅱 ©

The village stands on a windy hill a mile from the canal at Goldstone Wharf. The 13th century church is particularly delightful. Shops include a butcher, baker and Moore's Stores (open 6.30am–1pm and 2pm–8pm Mon–Sat and 8am–1pm Sun) which has fresh bread, cakes and pies daily. There are two pubs; *The Red Lion* is a Marston's house, whilst the *Fox & Hounds* is a free house with evening meals (including curry on Thur) and Sunday lunches. Stock at the Post Office includes batteries, films and cards and it is open every day except Sunday, but beware Wednesday lunch break, which extends from 12.30 until 4pm! One of the most popular inns on the 'Shroppie', the *Wharf Tavern* (01630 661226) lies beside Bridge 55. It has changed out of all recognition since L.T.C. Rolt made his dreamlike visit in 1939, and now boasts a good choice of beers, and a full restaurant and grill room service.

## Bridges 53–48

Luxuriant farmland falls away to the west. From Bridge 53 it is a pleasant walk to *Goldstone Hall* (01630 661202) a restaurant serving fine food, including specialities such as lobster, booking is advisable.

Robin Smithett

**Waiting to enter Tyrley Top Lock alongside the wharf.**

## MAP 14
### Tyrley to Goldstone

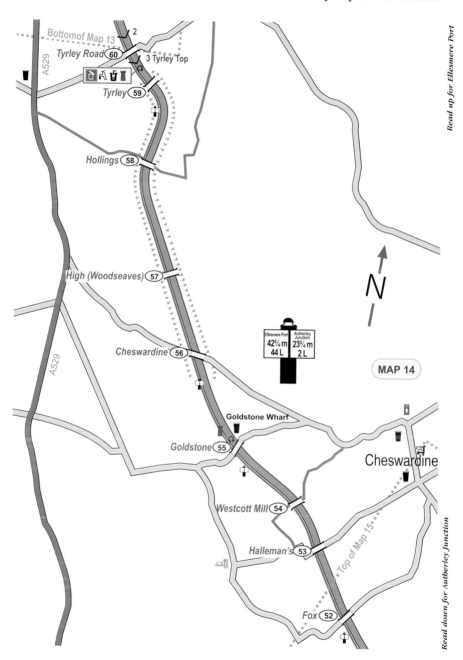

Read up for Ellesmere Port

Bottom of Map 13  2

Tyrley Road 60

A529

3 Tyrley Top

Tyrley 59

Hollings 58

High (Woodseaves) 57

Cheswardine 56

A529

| Ellesmere Port | Autherley Junction |
|---|---|
| 42¾ m | 23¾ m |
| 44 L | 2 L |

N

MAP 14

Goldstone Wharf

Goldstone 55

Cheswardine

Westcott Mill 54

Halleman's 53

Top of Map 15

Fox 52

Read down for Autherley Junction

## Soudley ▮

A tiny village about a mile from either Bridge 48 or 52. The *Wheatsheaf Inn* offers a warm welcome and is a Marston's house serving bar meals.

## Knighton ▮

At the northern end of Shebdon Embankment is one of the most poignant sights on the Shropshire Union: the wharf built with Cadbury's dried milk factory. The last cargo left here in the early 'sixties and yet the wharf is in excellent condition, although part has been walled off from the canal. The factory with its fine Art Deco tower, is now operated by Premier Foods and busies itself with the manufacture of Marvel and drinking chocolate, and the cargoes go on lorries bludgeoning their way down the country lanes. Half a mile down the hill is a pub, the *Haberdashers' Arms*, a free house with Banks' ales, a garden and a children's play area. It is open all day, everyday but not before 5pm on Wednesdays. Underwater boulders make mooring near Bridges 45–46 challenging.

## Shebdon Embankment ▮

One of the great 'Shroppie' embankments. Trees, originally planted to stabilise the bank and provide timber for maintenance work, hide the surrounding landscape, but if they didn't shelter the canal, navigating this length on a windy day would be extremely difficult. At the southern end of the embankment the canal crosses a country lane. The wharf here was once busy; there's still a winding hole maintained by the private owner who asks boats not to make contact with the sides and, nestling at the foot of the bank, the *Wharf Inn* with bar meals, a games room and garden but closed on Mondays and only open from 6pm Mon–Sat plus Sunday lunchtime and evening.

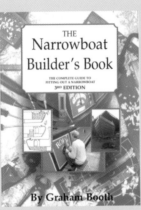

# MAP 15
## Soudley to Shebdon Aqueduct

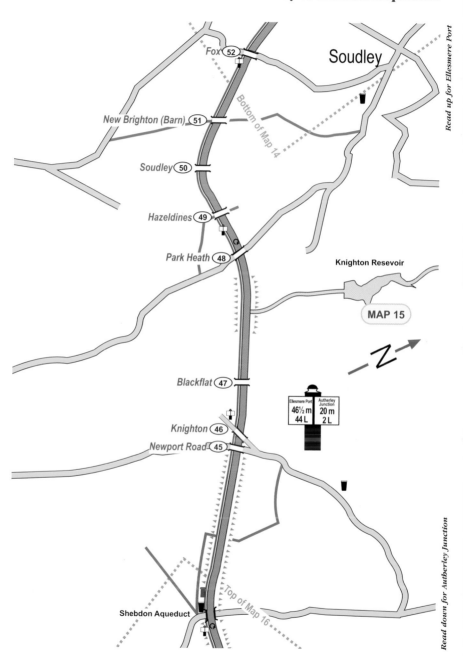

Read up for Ellesmere Port

Fox (52)

Soudley

New Brighton (Barn) (51)

Bottom of Map 14

Soudley (50)

Hazeldines (49)

Park Heath (48)

Knighton Resevoir

MAP 15

N

Blackflat (47)

| Ellesmere Port | Autherley Junction |
|---|---|
| 46½ m | 20 m |
| 44 L | 2 L |

Knighton (46)

Newport Road (45)

Shebdon Aqueduct

Top of Map 16

Read down for Autherley Junction

The spectacular cuttings of the southern part of the Shropshire Union Main Line demand some equally spectacular bridges, even to carry comparatively minor roads over the waterway. High Bridge (39) in Grub Street Cutting is braced to resist the inward pressure from the cutting sides.

*Robin Smitbett*

## Bridge 42–41

*The Anchor Inn* (01785 284569) by Bridge 42 has been in the Cliff family for over a hundred years. It has hardly changed from the old boatman's pub known as 'Lily Pascall's' that it once was. From Easter until October it's normal pub hours, but only on Fri–Sun lunch in winter. Sandwiches are made to order. Marstons Pedigree, 6X, Owd Roger and Barley Wine are on draught and a dozen different ciders are available. There are also camping/caravanning facilities including static units for hire and a gift shop selling canalware, pottery, postcards and Anchor Inn Tee-shirts/sweatshirts.

## High Offley ▌ ⓒ

The squat tower of High Offley's 15th century church stands at the top of its hill

to the south-east. The village can be reached from either bridge 41 or 42.

## Grub Street Cutting

The A519 Eccleshall–Newport road crosses the canal on the famous High Bridge with its unusual double arch. The lower arch is a later addition acting as a strengthening buttress. For about a mile the canal is completely enclosed by dense vegetation; one half expects to meet Bogart, Hepburn and the *African Queen* around the next bend!

## Norbury Junction
▬ ▌ ⓒ ⩑ ⛟ ▣ ▌

Norbury village is actually about ½ mile from the canal, but a self-contained little community has blossomed around the

# MAP 16
## Shebdon to Norbury

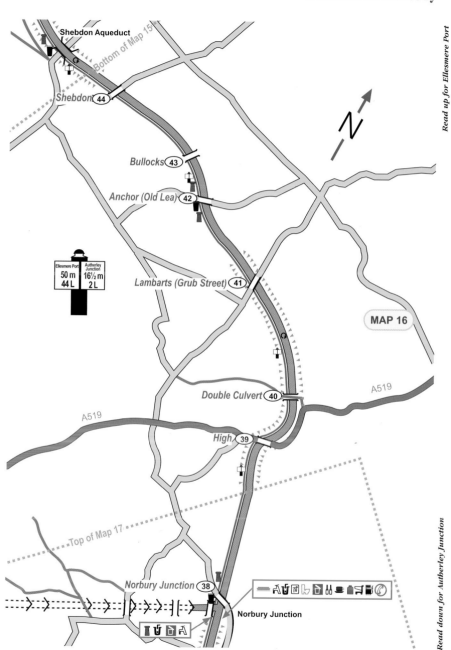

Shebdon Aqueduct

Bottom of Map 15

Shebdon 44

Bullocks 43

Anchor (Old Lea) 42

| Ellesmere Port | Autherley Junction |
|---|---|
| 50 m | 16½ m |
| 44 L | 2 L |

Lambarts (Grub Street) 41

MAP 16

A519

Double Culvert 40

A519

High 39

Top of Map 17

Norbury Junction 38

Norbury Junction

canal maintenance yard and, latterly, the boatyard. Sadly, 'Junction' is nowadays a misnomer for the canal that went westwards to Shrewsbury was closed in 1944 although there is pressure for restoration. But Norbury Junction, a spick and span little place where even the bridges are whitewashed, has lost none of its 'busyness', and a short length of the Shrewsbury & Newport Canal, giving access to a drydock, remains to give at least the illusion of a junction. The British Waterways yard (01785 284253) looks after the canal under supervision from the Birmingham Office. The *Junction Inn* (01785 284288) is a free house with bar meals every lunchtime and evening in summer (when the pub is open all day) but only at weekends in winter.

**Anglo-Welsh Waterway Holidays**
Norbury Junction (01785 284292) ▬

🗮 🛢 ⚒ 🛥 🛢 🛒 🛢 🛈 ⊘ 🍴 🎿 🍺

*solid fuels, chandlery, hire craft, servicing, repairs, boat painting, Boat Safety Scheme inspections, breakdowns, boatbuilding, wet & dry docks, slipway, shop & off licence. There's also a handy post box.* Anglo-Welsh also operate from Bunbury Locks and other bases. Hire craft (including day hire) details are available from 0117 304 1122 and www.anglowelsh.co.uk.

## Shelmore Embankment

This huge, mile-long embankment makes less of an impact on today's boater because of the trees which have grown up on either side, effectively preventing one from appreciating just how high above the surrounding farmland the canal actually is. But what a stark and uncompromising sight it must have been when new. No wonder that people then complained about the canal's intrusion on the countryside as we complain at yet another motorway. The embankment took a troublesome 5½ years to build; indeed, at times there were up to 600 men and 70 horses working on it. It was the last section

of the Shropshire Union to be finished, being completed in 1835. It is said that the difficulties contributed to the decline in Telford's health – he did not live to see the opening day. Extensive repairs have been carried out on the embankment over the winter of 2002–3 but traditionalists have critisised the use of steel pilings along such a notoriously unstable structure, which they say will tend to cut it apart and concentrate leaks. British Waterways engineers say they have prevented the possibility of overtopping in places where boat wash had eroded the banks and that they have created useful moorings.

## Bridges 36–37

The canal rides along an embankment and to the west the Wrekin – 1,335ft high – can be seen 15 miles away on the far side of Telford new town. If you can't see it the chances are that it's either going to be very hot or very wet!

## Gnosall Heath and Gnosall

(Say them with a silent G). *All services. Early Closing Wed.* Gnosall Heath has grown up beside the canal. *The Navigation* by Bridge 35 is a Pubmaster house, food is available and there's a garden and play area. Near Bridge 35 is a small Co-Op store open 8am–8pm Mon–Sat and 9am–1pm Sun. Access to Gnosall can be had from either Bridge 34 or 35 – it's about 15 minutes walk into the village and there's a variety of shops, and a Barclays Bank (open 10am–2.30pm, closed Tues). The Post Office sells stationery and gifts, and also has a dairy counter. *The Royal Oak* has Greene King, Abbott, Inde Coope and Tetley beers and food every lunch time and evening. Buses run to Stafford and Newport. There is a useful row of shops, including bakery and off licence, by Bridge 34, where Marstons' *Boat Inn* with its curious curved wall is situated. Home-cooked food is served lunchtime and evening, Mon–Sat with a special menu for the over 60s.

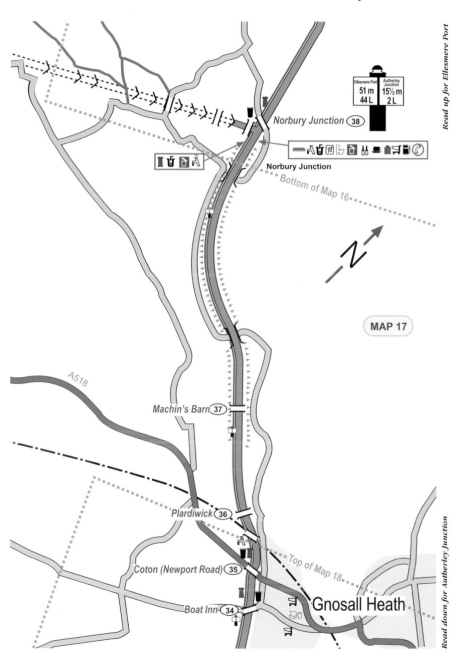

## MAP 17
### Norbury to Gnosall

Read up for Ellesmere Port

Ellesmere Port  Autherley Junction
51 m   15½ m
44 L   2 L

Norbury Junction (38)

Norbury Junction

Bottom of Map 16

MAP 17

A518

Machin's Barn (37)

Plardiwick (36)

Coton (Newport Road) (35)

Top of Map 18

Boat Inn (34)

Gnosall Heath

Read down for Autherley Junction

## Cowley Cutting

Climaxing with passing through the unlined 81 yards of Cowley Tunnel, the canal is cut through solid sandstone. In the mid-eighties, protruding tree roots caused concern about instability of the cutaway rock face, necessitating removal of all the overhanging foliage. Nature is taking over again, however, and grass and wild flowers grow once more on the sheer sides of the cutting.

## Bridges 31–28

A beautiful tree-clad cutting, punctuated by handsome stone bridges. At points the overhead branches interleave to form a tracery ceiling.

**Bridge 26** is a good example of a 'roving bridge' used, in the days of horsedrawn boats, to enable the horses to cross the canal with the towpath without need to unhitch the towline.

## Church Eaton ⓒ🍺

The village lies a mile east of High Onn Wharf.

**Passing the *Boat Inn* at Gnosall look out for its curiously curved wall.**

Robin Smithett

# MAP 18
## Gnosall to Little Onn

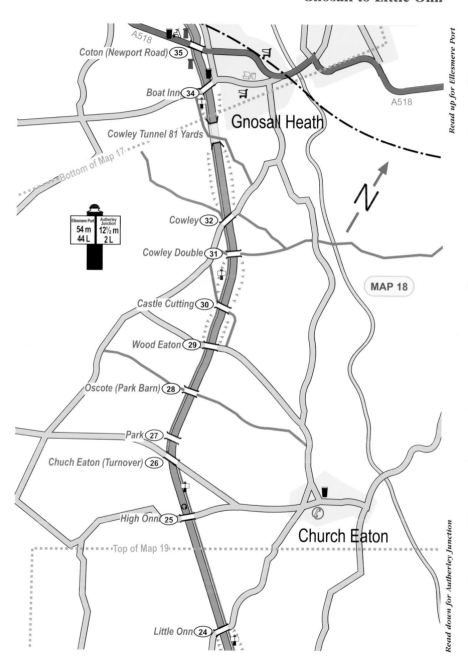

Robin Smitbett

**Thomas Telford is well known to canal enthusiasts for his work on the Shropshire Union and other waterways, perhaps less so for his skill in road building despite the two meeting at Stretton Aqueduct.**

## Bridges 24–20

The canal runs through wooded cuttings alternating with long straights with good views to the east towards Cannock Chase.

## Wheaton Aston 🚶 🍽 🏠 🏪 ♿ 🛢 🛈

A straggling, largely residential, village of little interest to the canal traveller except for its facilities. The *Hartley Arms* (01785 840232) by Bridge 19 serves Banks' and guest traditional ales, and offers huge platesful of home-cooked food all day, every day. Across the lane is Turner's garage which seems to do as much business with boats as with motor cars! The Garage has a little side store selling solid fuel, bottled gas, films, postcards and ice cream, some essential chandlery such as mooring spikes and windlasses and all types of 'consumables' for the engine.

At the far end of the village (about 10 mins walk) is Banks' *Coach & Horses*, a huge old coaching inn. Down by the church is a Spar grocery open 8.30am–9.30pm Mon–Sat, 10am–2pm Sun.

## Bridge 19–15

South of Wheaton Aston wharf with its useful facilities is the last, or first, serious lock on the Birmingham & Liverpool Junction section of the Shropshire Union. This is also the deepest with its 7ft change of level thus ensuring that each boat would send enough water down towards Tyrley to fill the following locks. Above the lock Lapley Wood shades another cutting.

## MAP 19
### High Onn to Wheaton Aston

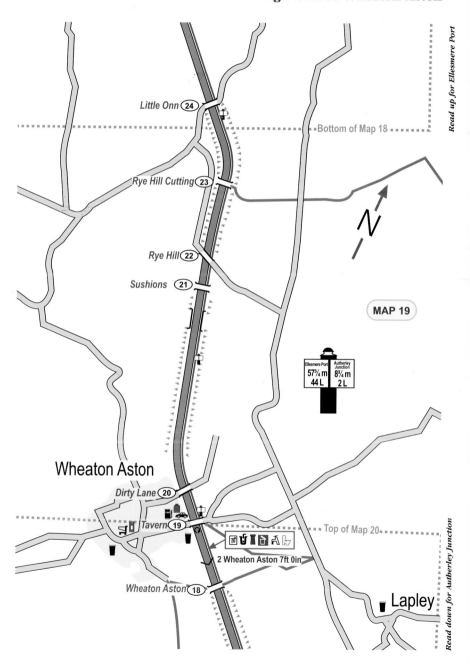

Read up for Ellesmere Port

Little Onn (24)

Bottom of Map 18

Rye Hill Cutting (23)

N

Rye Hill (22)

Sushions (21)

MAP 19

Ellesmere Port | Autherley Junction
57¾ m | 8¾ m
44 L | 2 L

Wheaton Aston

Dirty Lane (20)

Tavern (19)

Top of Map 20

2 Wheaton Aston 7ft 0in

Wheaton Aston (18)

Lapley

Read down for Autherley Junction

*Euan Corrie*

**Brewood is a useful source of sustenance and supplies as well as being an attractive village with convenient moorings towards the southern end of the Shropshire Union.**

A walk from Bridge 17 could lead to the *Vaughan Arms* in Lapley village where beers are Marston's and Banks' and food is served both lunchtime and evening.

Thomas Telford's exquisite aqueduct of 1832 carries the Shropshire Union Canal over the A5 road, itself reconstructed to Telford's designs in 1830 from an old coaching turnpike running on the line of the Roman Watling Street.

Between bridges 15 ands 16 on the off-side is Homestead Caravan Park (01902 851302) with holiday caravan homes for sale and hire and a heated indoor pool in its leisure club.

## Brewood  *All Services.*
*Early Closing Wed*

A snug village, dating from Roman times. perched on a peaceful hill away from Watling Street's hurrying traffic. The locals call it 'Brood'. It has associations with the fugitive Charles II, who hid high up in an oak tree at nearby Boscobel

while the Cromwellians searched below. Colonel Carless, a local man who assisted Charles in his escape, is buried in the graveyard of the parish church of St. Mary and St. Chad.

By Bridge 14 the *Bridge Inn* (01902 851999), open all day except Sun when it closes at 4pm, serves Burtonwood beers and food for which you are advised to book at weekends. It also aims to be dog and walker friendly! Opposite the church is the *Moghal-E-Azam* Bangladeshi Restaurant (01902 850989). Down the hill from the church is the locally recommended *Admiral Rodney* (01902 850583), a charming pub, open all day at weekends, decorated in Victorian style and serving Anglo-Italian food every lunchtime and evening with barbecues on Sat & Sun evenings. Among the beers on sale here are Adnams Broadside, Marston's Pedigree and changing guests. Children are welcome and there is a large garden with games including a putting

# MAP 20
## Wheaton Aston to Brewood

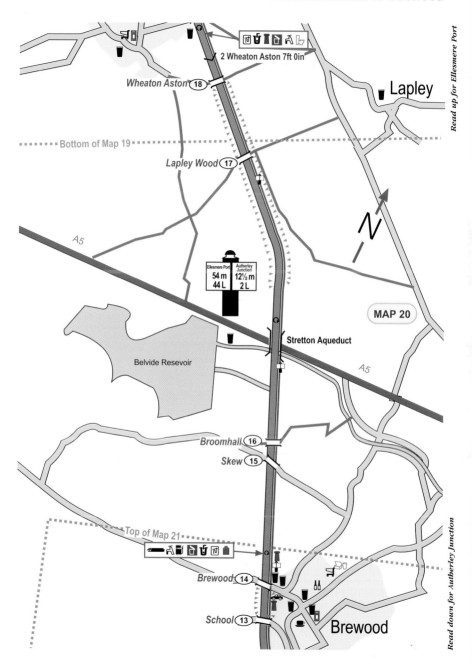

Read up for Ellesmere Port

2 Wheaton Aston 7ft 0in

Wheaton Aston 18

Lapley

Bottom of Map 19

Lapley Wood 17

A5

| Ellesmere Port | Autherley Junction |
|---|---|
| 54 m | 12½ m |
| 44 L | 2 L |

MAP 20

Stretton Aqueduct

A5

Belvide Resevoir

Broomhall 16

Skew 15

Top of Map 21

Brewood 14

School 13

Brewood

Read down for Autherley Junction

green. In the Market Place the *Connoisseur* tea rooms is open every day but only at lunchtime on Sunday. A carvery is offered on Thur–Sat evenings with an a la carte menu on Friday evening. Overlooking The Square is *The Swan* with Courage Directors and Theakstons as well as guest ales. Food is served at lunchtime except on Sundays and Folk music is played on Thursdays. *Stirrups* offers food every day except Monday and entertainment on Friday and Saturday evenings; it's open all day, every day. The PO/stores is open on Sunday mornings. Next door is the *Lion Hotel*.

Down Stafford Street is Maiden's, the oldest shop in Brewood, which is still run by the Maiden family. It is a butcher, greengrocer and grocer and sells delicious home made pies (open Mon–Sat). On Tues, Thur, Fri and Sat fresh fish is available. Opposite is a useful Spar general store, which stays open until 10pm. At the bottom of the street is a Chinese takeaway/fish & chip shop.

**Countrywide Cruisers** (01902 850166) ▦ ▦ ♨ ⚓ ■ ▱ ▣ *hire craft, boatbuilding, fitting out, maps and guides, repairs and servicing, slipway.* Note that, unusually on the canals, all these services are charged for. Countrywide are members of the Blue Riband Club.

**Bridge 10** The ornamental balustrades of this bridge give a clue to its origin. To the west lies 18th century Chillington Hall (01902 850236), which is open on Easter Sunday, other Sundays before Bank Holidays, Thur–Sun in July and Wed–Sun in August. As with many canals, the local landowner would only permit the new trade route to cross his land if the ugly reality of its commercial nature was suitably disguised.

## Bridges 8–4

The canal passes through two narrow rock cuttings where there is insufficient room for craft to pass. The adjoining fields roll away to either horizon with

*kevin Maslin*

**Avenue Bridge: The new eye-sore of the Birmingham & Liverpool Junction Canal main line cut through the park at Chillington Hall and in an attempt to make this desecration as acceptable as possible the bridge carrying the main carriage drive over the cut was the most ornamental on the route.**

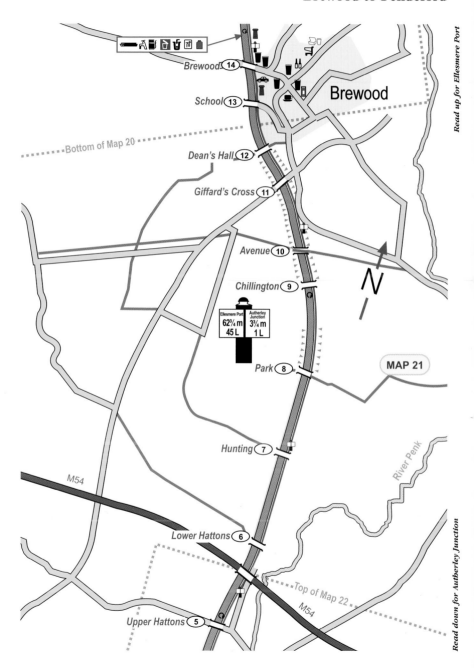

MAP 21
**Brewood to Pendeford**

Read up for Ellesmere Port

Brewood ⑭

Brewood

School ⑬

Bottom of Map 20

Dean's Hall ⑫

Giffard's Cross ⑪

Avenue ⑩

Chillington ⑨

N

| Ellesmere Port | Autherley Junction |
|---|---|
| 62¾ m | 3¾ m |
| 45 L | 1 L |

Park ⑧

MAP 21

Hunting ⑦

River Penk

M54

Lower Hattons ⑥

Top of Map 22

M54

Upper Hattons ⑤

Read down for Autherley Junction

Peter Ivermee

**The arches of many of the Shropshire Union's bridges certainly needed their iron protection from the continual passage of horse towing lines which gradually wore these deep grooves. Imagine the damage whgich would have been caused to an unprotected brick arch.**

here and there a group of isolated red-brick farm buildings. The M54 motorway crosses the canal here. Uphill from Bridge 4 is a useful local centre with pub, shops and Post Office.

**Wolverhampton Boat Club** has its moorings between Bridges 3 and 4. They are a friendly club and welcome boaters to their licensed clubhouse, which is open on Wed, Fri, Sat, Sun evenings and Sun lunchtimes.

Between Bridge 3 and Autherley Junction there is public open space bordering the housing which covers the site of Wolverhampton's airport. Five or ten minutes' walk along the road will bring you to a Safeway supermarket, a Post Office and an M&B pub – *The Pendulum* – which serves food at lunchtimes and evenings every day.

## Autherley Junction

On the northern outskirts of Wolverhampton the Shropshire Union Canal forms a junction with the Staffordshire & Worcestershire Canal. The shallow stop lock was installed to separate the two companies' water supplies. The

formerly convenient Elsan point has been moved three-quarters of the way to Bridge 2; curious until you look through the hedge and discover Wolverhampton's Barnhurst Sewage Works.

**Water Travel** (01902 782371, www. water-travel.co.uk) *solid fuel, chandlery, canalia, books, maps and guides, hire craft, boatbuilding, repairs and servicing, slipway,* Closed Sundays.

**Oxley Marina** On the Staffs & Worcs Canal (01902 789522) *solid fuel, slipway, servicing and repairs, chandlery, maps and guides, solid fuel, boatbuilding, engine repairs, Boat Safety Scheme inspections arranged, craft shop, boat brokerage, public and charter trip boat.* There is a licenced club on the premises to which visitors are welcomed every evening all year for a peaceful chat and a pint.

Turning left out of the Stop Lock at Autherley, or 'Cut End' as the working boat people knew it, leads to the Staffordshire & Worcestershire Canal towards Great Haywood. To the right, past Oxley Marina a half-mile cutting leads to Aldersley Junction at the bottom of the Birmingham Canal's 21 Wolverhampton Locks. Ahead, from there, is the Staffordshire & Worcestershire Canal to Stourport.

The *Waterways World Guide to the Staffs & Worcs Canal* describes the route from Great Haywood, junction with the Trent & Mersey Canal, to Stourport-on-Severn.

# MAP 22
## Pendeford to Wolverhampton

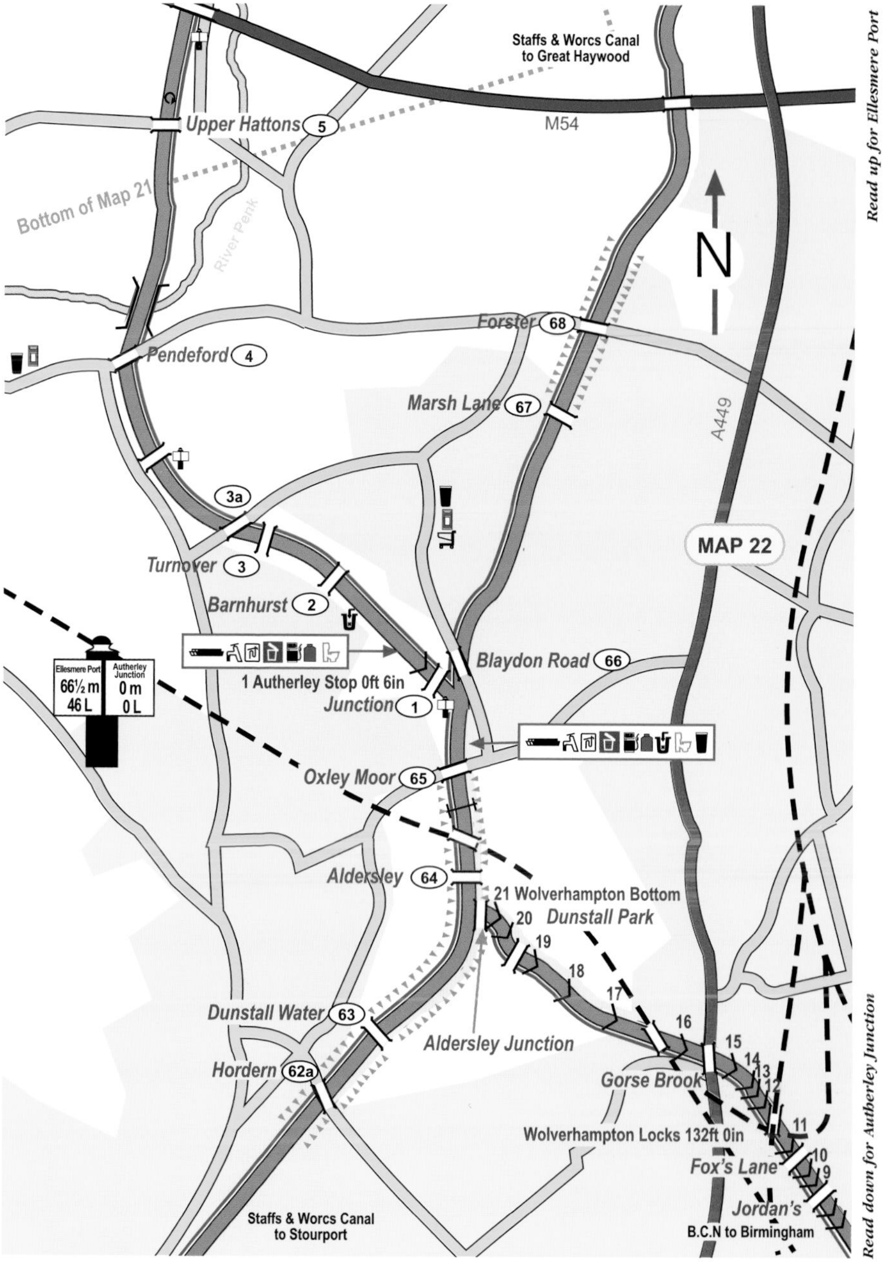

Staffs & Worcs Canal to Great Haywood
M54
Upper Hattons (5)
Bottom of Map 21
River Penk
Forster (68)
Pendeford (4)
Marsh Lane (67)
A449
N
3a
MAP 22
Turnover (3)
Barnhurst (2)
Blaydon Road (66)
Ellesmere Port 66½ m 46 L
Autherley Junction 0 m 0 L
1 Autherley Stop 0ft 6in
Junction (1)
Oxley Moor (65)
Aldersley (64)
21 Wolverhampton Bottom
20 Dunstall Park
19
18
17
16
15
14
13
12
11
10
9
Dunstall Water (63)
Aldersley Junction
Hordern (62a)
Gorse Brook
Wolverhampton Locks 132ft 0in
Fox's Lane
Jordan's
B.C.N to Birmingham
Staffs & Worcs Canal to Stourport
Read up for Ellesmere Port
Read down for Autherley Junction

*The Ellesmere and Chester canals having amalgamated, a much-needed link to the Trent & Mersey at Middlewich was completed in 1833 in anticipation of the through route of the Birmingham & Liverpool Junction.*

## Barbridge Junction

This is the junction of the Shropshire Union's Main Line and its Middlewich Branch, it is fully described on page 34. A long length of moorings opens the quiet rural journey to Middlewich and the Trent & Mersey Canal.

**Barbridge Marina (Midway Boats Ltd)** (01270 528682) *solid fuel, servicing and repairs, slipway up to 30ft, boat sales and brokerage, chandlery, Boat Safety Scheme inspections, boat and engine repairs and breakdowns, outboard sales and servicing, boat transport.*

Other facilities for boats and boat people are described on page 34.

As the Middlewich Branch leaves Barbridge its style is established almost immediately, passing through lush pastureland supporting rich dairy farms the route is peaceful, avoiding main roads. The locks are deeper than on the narrow section of the Shropshire Union Main line and fill more fiercely as a result, so do not open gate paddles too early when ascending for fear of flooding your foredeck. Below Cholmondeston Lock is the uncharacteristic hive of activity which is Venetian Marina.

**Venetian Marine (Nantwich) Ltd** (01270 528251, www.vanetianmarina. co.uk) *brokerage*. Venetian Marine operates the marina itself, which is host to other businesses:

**Kate's Canal Shop** (01270 528151) is immediately obvious on the water's edge at Venetian Marina. They can provide, or direct you to: *solid fuels, second hand books and souvenirs every day of the week.*

**Bake 'n' Butty** (01270 528752) is just around the corner if your need is more in terms of all-day breakfasts, homemade cakes, Cheshire farm ice cream or many similar mouth-watering essentials.

**Aquafax** (01270 528822) will be found even further round the corner! However, Aquafax may not be a well known name since they deal in bulk wholesale supply of chandlery and boat builders equipment and do not aim to offer a general retail service.

**R.J. Marine** (01270 528787) is at the far side of Venetian Marina's buildings where they provide boat building and maintenance services. *slipway, boat building, fitting out, painting and boat and engine repairs. They can arrange cranage and Boat Safety Scheme inspections, but cannot cater for DIY works.*

## Bridges 5–8

Beyond Venetian Marina the former London & North Western Railway branch from Crewe to Chester, which follows the Shropshire Union main line below Bunbury, strides across on an embankment. In the cutting beyond the railway is an extensive clay pit with a hut on the towpath which provided shelter for those employed to dig clay for repairs to the canal lining.

The cottage at Minshull Lock was destroyed by fire a few years ago and has been rebuilt with remarkable restraint to match the original.

**MAP 23**

### Middlewich Branch  Barbridge to Minshull

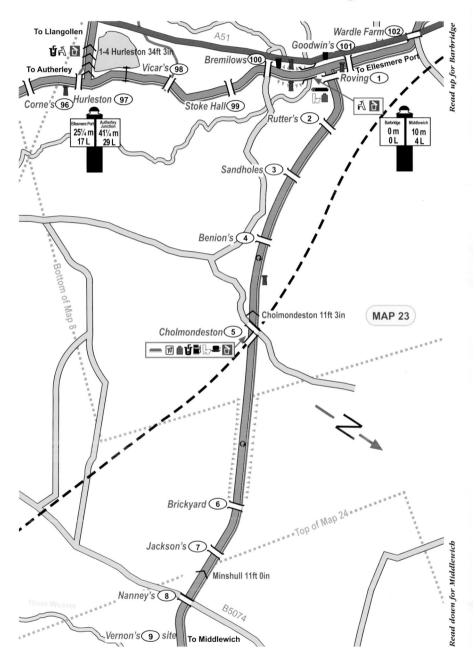

To Llangollen

1-4 Hurleston 34ft 3in

To Autherley

Vicar's 98

*A51*

Goodwin's 101

Wardle Farm 102

Bremilows 100

To Ellesmere Port

Roving 1

Corne's 96

Hurleston 97

Stoke Hall 99

Rutter's 2

| Ellesmere Port | Autherley Junction |
|---|---|
| 25¼ m | 41¼ m |
| 17 L | 29 L |

| Barbridge | Middlewich |
|---|---|
| 0 m | 10 m |
| 0 L | 4 L |

Sandholes 3

Benion's 4

Cholmondeston 11ft 3in

MAP 23

Bottom of Map 8

Cholmondeston 5

N

Brickyard 6

Top of Map 24

Jackson's 7

Minshull 11ft 0in

Nanney's 8

B5074

River Weaver

Vernon's 9 site

To Middlewich

Read up for Barbridge

Read down for Middlewich

## Bridges 8–14

The canal makes an exciting crossing of the river Weaver on a high embankment above a three-arched aqueduct. To the east lies a 'dry valley', the geographers' term for a valley with no stream or river running through it. What has happened here, and in similar cases, is that the original watercourse will have, at some point in the geological past, disappeared underground.

## Church Minshull ▌ ℭ

This is the village of which L.T.C. Rolt wrote so fondly in *Narrow Boat*. Sixty years on, it still contains 'many excellent examples of the timber-framed houses built in genuine regional style', but he would have been disappointed at the absence of local craftsmen, the dereliction of the mill, and the volume of traffic on the rural lanes. Whatever's been lost, is compensated for by the friendly villagers and the *Badger Inn* where there's real ale, food every lunchtime and evening and large-screen TV. A Crewe–Northwich bus service runs through the village; the bus stop is by the interesting 18th century Church of St Bartholomew. Church Minshull is famous in angling circles for the annual Nantwich Round Table fishing match, held on the canal hereabouts in October. The old Dutch-gabled wharf house is now a private dwelling, mooring in front of which is prohibited.

## Bridges 15–22

The canal clings to a shelf high above Winsford Top Flash on the river Weaver – the views are tremendous. A mile downstream is the bigger Bottom Flash, the head of navigation on the Weaver, a 20-mile waterway linking Winsford with the Manchester Ship Canal at Weston Point. As recently as the 1930s there were serious proposals to extend navigation of the river through here to Audlem whence a 100-ton barge-sized Shropshire Union would have linked to Wolverhampton.

*Robin Smitbett*

**Wardle Lock.**

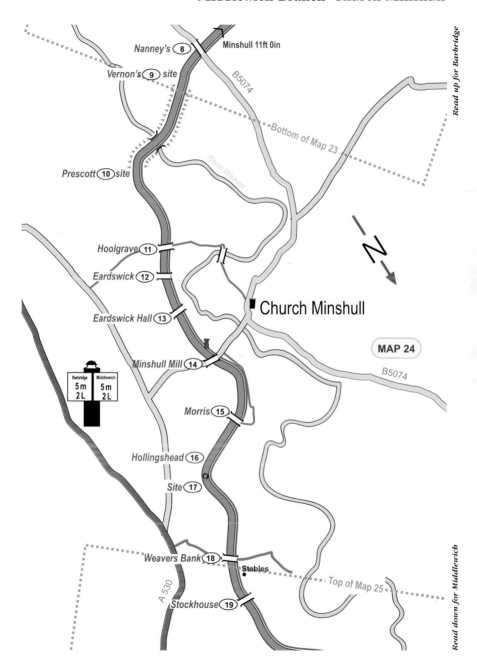

**MAP 24**

**Middlewich Branch  Church Minshull**

Nanney's (8)   Minshull 11ft 0in

Vernon's (9) site

B5074

Read up for Barbridge

Bottom of Map 23

Prescott (10) site

River Weaver

N

Hoolgrave (11)

Eardswick (12)

Eardswick Hall (13)

■ Church Minshull

**MAP 24**

B5074

Minshull Mill (14)

| Barbridge | Middlewich |
|-----------|------------|
| 5 m<br>2 L | 5 m<br>2 L |

Morris (15)

Hollingshead (16)

Site (17)

Weavers Bank (18)   Stables

A 530

Top of Map 25

Read down for Middlewich

Stockhouse (19)

## Bridges 23–26

Winsford railway station – local trains between Crewe and Liverpool – is only a mile down either lane to the north-west. Bridge 22A carries the quadruple tracked Euston–Glasgow main line of the former LNWR. Alas Stanier's Pacifics are no more, but many of the electric locomotives carry names. A short section of the Middlewich Branch was the scene of an unusual experiment in 1888. A narrow gauge railway was built along the towpath, and little steam locomotives (normally used to convey materials around Crewe Works) were employed in hauling narrowboats in place of the horses hitherto used. Unfortunately, the trials proved unsuccessful but it was a form of motive power that did catch on abroad.

## Bridges 27–28

Below Stanthorne Lock an embankment carries the canal over the A530 and the river Wheelock.

## Middlewich  *All Services.*

A Cheshire salt town – the suffix 'wich' is old English for salt. The Romans discovered salt here and called the town Salinae. Salt is still an important industry in the town, albeit the modern vacuum method has replaced the 'open pan'. The townscape is dominated by the perpendicular Parish Church of St Michael, and there's a good choice of shops within easy reach of the canal.

Full details of Middlewich are given in the *Waterways World Guide to the Trent & Mersey Canal*. However, good moorings are to be had upstream of Bridge 31 on the branch and there is a water point on the Trent & Mersey just upstream of Bridge 168. There is also a general store nearby, pubs, a fish & chip bar and space to wind in the 'T' of the junction. There are two boatyards located on the Trent & Mersey through Bridge 168. Incidentally,

the bridge bears a stone inscribed 'Wardle Canal 1829', reminding that this was originally a short arm off the T & M, the Shropshire Union proper beginning above the lock because the Trent & Mersey Canal Act prohibited other companies from making a direct connection to that canal's main line.

Both Barclays and NatWest have banks in Wheelock Street where Dillons supermarket (and post office) is also located – open daily 8am–10pm. *The King's Lock* overlooking King's Lock on the Trent & Mersey Canal by the junction offers Tetleys ales and home cooked food every lunchtime and evening. *The Cheshire Cheese*, on the main road behind Middlewich Narrowboats close to Bridge 169, has Sky TV while going over Bridge 169 leads to a short walk downhill to the *Boar's Head* where Robinson's beers may be enjoyed as well as restaurant and bar food lunchtime and evening Wed–Sun. There is also B&B accommodation. Below the three locks down the Trent & Mersey is the *Newton Brewery Inn*, a Marston's house offering home cooked food every day including Sunday lunch and eves and the *Big Lock*, by Lock 75. This is a refurbished Marston's pub with a dining room, a la carte menu and bar meals and snacks available 7 days a week, lunch time and eves. About 100 yards to the north of Bridge 172 is the *Kinderton House Hotel* whose restaurant is given three crowns by the English Tourist Board. Booking advisable (01606 833191).

**King's Lock Boatyard** on the Trent & Mersey directly opposite the junction (01606 737564, www.kingslock.fsnet.co.uk) 🏠 ⛽ 🛥 *solid fuel, well-stocked chandlery, slipway, boat and engine repairs including breakdowns.*

**L.A. Boat Joinery** (07976 683966) fits out boats at King's Lock Boatyard.

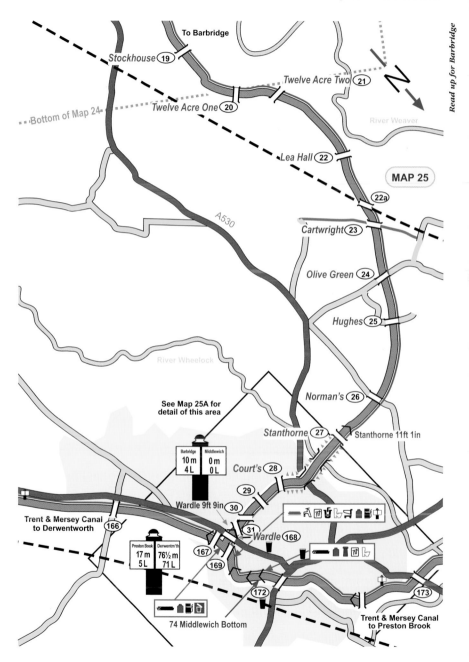

MAP 25

Middlewich Branch  Wimboldsey to Middlewich

To Barbridge

Read up for Barbridge

Stockhouse (19)

Twelve Acre Two (21)

Bottom of Map 24

Twelve Acre One (20)

River Weaver

Lea Hall (22)

MAP 25

(22a)

A530

Cartwright (23)

Olive Green (24)

Hughes (25)

River Wheelock

Norman's (26)

See Map 25A for
detail of this area

Stanthorne (27)   Stanthorne 11ft 1in

| Barbridge | Middlewich |
|---|---|
| 10 m | 0 m |
| 4 L | 0 L |

Court's (28)

(29)

Wardle 9ft 9in (30)

Trent & Mersey Canal
to Derwentworth (166)

(31)

Wardle (168)

| Preston Book | Derwentm'th |
|---|---|
| 17 m | 76½ m |
| 5 L | 71 L |

(167)

(169)

(172)

(173)

74 Middlewich Bottom

Trent & Mersey Canal
to Preston Brook

**Middlewich Narrowboats** At the wharf on the Trent & Mersey to the left (downstream) of the junction. (01606 832460, www.middlewichboats.co.uk) *solid fuel, chandlery, canalia, books, maps and guides, serviced laundry (weekdays), hire craft (especially traditional style ones for*

*larger groups), boat repairs and servicing, breakdown service.*

**Andersen Boats** Below Middlewich Three Locks on the Trent & Mersey to the left of the junction (01606 833668, www.andersenboats.com) *hire craft.*

## MAP 25A
## Middlewich (Detail)

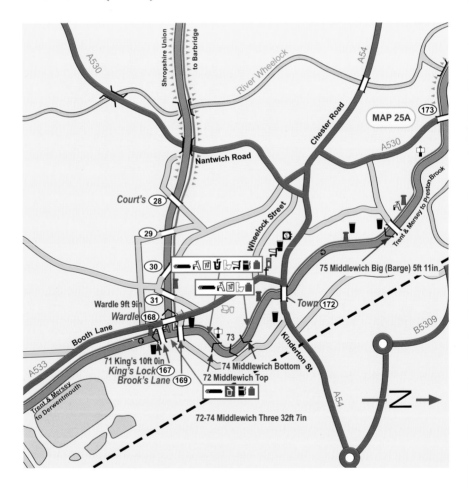

------------------------------------------- Fold along dotted line and seal open edges before mailing -------------

No stamp
needed

**Canal Guides Editor**
**Waterways World Ltd**
**Freepost MID20568**
**Burton-on-Trent**
**DE14 1BR**

# Help us to Update

We've made every effort to ensure that this edition of the Waterways World Guide to the Shropshire Union Canal is accurate and up-to-date. However, things change – new facilities are offered, opening hours are notoriously fickle, pub ownership and names change. If you feel we've got it wrong or left something out, we'd like to know. You can use this pre-paid return form to let us know the correct information. Please give details in the space below and return to WW Guides Editor or e-mail admin@wwonline.co.uk.

Place:                                              Date:

Details of change:

Place:                                              Date:

Details of change:

Place:                                              Date:

Details of change: